WHY DEMOCRACY MATTERS

WHY DEMOCRACY MATTERS

An introduction to
what the Bible says about
civil government

JOHN NORSWORTHY

Foreword by Lynn Arnold

Why Democracy Matters
Published by ConsultEd Publishing
45 Bathurst Crescent, Pyes Pa
Tauranga
New Zealand

© 2025 John Norsworthy

ISBN 978-0-473-76447-0 (Softcover)
ISBN 978-0-473-76445-6 (ePUB)
ISBN 978-0-473-76446-3 (Kindle)

Production & Typesetting:
Andrew Killick
Castle Publishing Services
www.castlepublishing.co.nz

Cover Design:
Paul Smith

Scriptures taken from the Holy Bible,
New International Version®, NIV®.
Copyright © 1973, 1978, 1984, 2011 by Biblica, Inc.™
Used by permission of Zondervan.
All rights reserved worldwide.

ALL RIGHTS RESERVED

No part of this publication may be reproduced,
stored in a retrieval system, or transmitted
in any form or by any means, electronic, mechanical,
photocopying, recording or otherwise,
without prior written permission from the author or publisher.

FOREWORD

John Norsworthy has established a credible reputation as an articulator of biblical foundations behind key contemporary issues. Having previously dealt with culture, science and humility in the Why Something Matters series, he has now taken on the issue of good governance, and in particular civil government.

A particular practical virtue of his writing style is that, in his own words, he keeps his writing simple, short and faithful. What this means for the reader is the experience of reading thoughtful, well-founded but not daunting extended essays on topics of importance for our contemporary world.

In this book, this style of writing and approach has been continued. The expectation of any reader in seeing such a title from an author who has a strong faith would be that the work would help give clarity to the interplay of such terms as democracy, governance, public square and the common good along with the overriding question of 'Where is God in all of this?' In the space of less than 300 pages, John Norsworthy has done all of this.

The book has been designed both for individual reading and group study and the biblical underpinnings are not only well chosen but very apt in terms of the theological lens through which he tackles the subject.

He finishes the book with a section which, for my part, is where I would suggest the reader start – namely about 60 discussion starters related to public life. Asking oneself, or a group, these questions before turning to the first page of the book could be a useful aid to enabling the contents of the fourteen chapters to rumble meaningfully in one's mind.

John's approach of faith to the question of civil government is prophetic rather than just reactive. A reactive approach to the topic would simply aim at societal stability, even just the creation of a comfort zone of acceptable societal cohesion amidst the diversity of community opinion and expectations. This work, however, is about exploring the project of being about our Father's business, kingdom-building here on earth. In this context, a prophetic approach seeks to foretell how things could be in terms of a deeper social cohesion that asks us to understand the more profound shared values the Bible calls us to seek.

To do that prophetic thought-provoking, this book starts with the biblical narratives about governance and civil society. Starting with a breath-taking run through the Hebrew Bible on the topic, he then moves to the New Testament commentary. This part occupies over half the text; but it is clearly important that so much space is devoted to that analysis as it creates the lens through which it then analyses subsequent historical and contemporary challenges of governance.

John's aim in creating such a lens is to enable a 'both and' rather than an 'either or' approach to questions of responsibility and accountability in the matter of governance in civil society. Governments should be responsible and accountable if there is to be good governance; but so too should be individuals and grassroots community. He does not let easy solutions to complex problems take hold in his analysis – 'oh, the government should do that' or 'it's purely a matter for individual responsibility' – rather, he wants to force us to consider the interplay of responsibilities and accountabilities between all of us as Godly-created social beings in Godly-ordained community.

If there is a point where the reader might take issue with John, it would be when he posits an uncomfortable thought about the role God might have had in raising up authoritarian governments.

There is a valid historical record of 'benedicta' (good word) versus 'dictadura' (hard word) involvement of authoritarian leadership – in the Roman Republic for example, or, even in contemporary times, in times of war. However, the question cannot be avoided that regimes like North Korea hardly seem compatible with a view of God's ordination. The dynamics of the sovereignty and goodness of God in the light of human suffering is a big topic. As big an issue as this is, however, John simply refers the reader back to thinking more deeply about what the Bible does call us to do in terms of our individual or grassroots roles in the face of unjust government – an issue which John certainly does deal with in many different parts of the book.

In summary, in these especially troubled and conflicted times, this book is very timely. We so need to be encouraged to reflect on its call to each of us, individually and collectively, to be about God's business of His Kingdom here on earth.

Rev. Dr. Lynn Arnold AO
Reader, St Barnabas Theological College,
Adelaide, South Australia

(Lynn Arnold has actively worked in many ways for social and political justice. He has been in leadership positions such as the Premier of South Australia, a Senior Director of World Vision International and Leader of Anglicare SA.)

CONTENTS

Preface 11

1. Taking Dominion and the Problem with Good and Evil 15
2. The Purpose of a God-fearing Nation 35
3. The Rule of God Through the Rule of Law 45
4. The Rise and Fall of a Nation 61
5. The Promised King 79
6. The Good News of the Kingdom of God 91
7. Identifying and Fixing the Problem 107
8. The Role of Government 129
9. Contrasting Kingdoms 139
10. Infiltrating and Overcoming 161
11. Believers and the Public Square 179
12. Addressing the Issues from a Biblical Perspective 205
13. What is It about Civil Government that Matters? 225

Group Discussion Starter Guide 245
Appendix: The New Zealand National Anthem 253
For Further Reading 257
Also by John Norsworthy 261

PREFACE

Those of us who live in the free world have had the privileged experience of living in an unprecedented prosperous and comparatively safe environment. This social and political context is showing signs of fragility. We urgently need to understand the nature of our times and so know what to do to preserve what we have. Amongst other privileges we have been able to express our opinions about an issue. This issue may involve science, religion, social justice, politics, community health, education, gender identity, family or any of a range of aspects of human life. This freedom to air our opinions is often taken for granted. Most of the time, before 'hate speech' legislation was mooted, it never crossed our mind of the possibility that we may be punished for expressing an opinion. In many places in the world freedom of speech is not assumed, especially if one seeks to speak about something that is political, or 'ideological'. Maybe we need to be reminded to celebrate and seek to defend this right of freedom to do things, to speak and to hear the opinions of others, even the speech of others with whom we disagree. How did this understanding of the right to be free from the oppression of others with social power develop? What framework of thinking birthed and nurtured this freedom? This book reminds us of the worldview behind the politics of the free world.

Over the years, I have worked with teachers in Christian schools. They have been keen to teach their subject or the topic in hand from a biblical perspective. Often, they have reported that they have realised that they really didn't know what the Bible had to say about the topic they were to teach. They often said that they tended to make the teaching and learning 'Christian' by teaching the topic in the standard 'secular' way and adding a scripture or two to represent a Christian perspective. Biblical literacy applied to all of life was often in short supply. I figured I could do my part in meeting this need. It was this quest to present a clear understanding of the biblical rationale behind a topic or practice that led me to write my previous books, and now to write this short book.

As a student of the Bible, I am disposed to ask the question, 'What does the Bible say?' I am convinced that the Bible, as the inspired Word of God, has something foundational to say, informing us about every issue in life. The Bible frames God's big picture story, the context in which an issue sits. If I gain some idea of what the biblical meta-narrative has to say about the issue, I gain confidence to make good decisions and pursue them with single-mindedness.

An enormous amount has been written on this topic of civil government. I do not plan to say something new but rather outline what I believe is some biblical teaching on the topic. I have attempted to confine myself to unpacking the scripture and its implications, the 'why' and the 'what' of a Christian approach to political involvement, rather than the 'how' to do such. As usual, I have reminded myself to keep it simple, keep it short and keep it faithful to the truth, so that someone new to the topic can get started on the path of understanding and involvement.

Over the years I have listened to and shared ideas with others. I am aware that they have read and studied the ideas of theologians and Christian thinkers such as Abraham Kuyper, Francis Schaeffer and Charles Colson and more recently N T Wright. My ideas have not usually come directly from reading these authors, and so I do not quote from them. Hence, there is not a list of references at the end, but a list of a few key books that will elaborate the concepts I have introduced. Inevitably, readers will see some things I write that are much like what they have heard before.

As this is not a book unpacking detailed historical facts, I deliberately make broad sweeping statements about historical movements. If you are a student or teacher of history and or theology, you do well not to just take my word for it, but rather do your own research and reading to confirm and to add detail to what I mention.

I am grateful to those who have critiqued drafts of this book and encouraged me in the process.

At the end of the book there are about 60 provocative statements related to the topic of Christians and public life. As Lynn Arnold suggests in the foreword, they can be used as thought provokers before you embark on reading. You could use them as questions to hook you in to finding wisdom as you read. On the other hand, they could be used by a group using the book as a base for a discussion series.

I trust that, as you read, you will be encouraged to seek out, discover and put into practice what God has called you to do for the kingdom of God, and explore your involvement in the public square.

In it all, we seek to see people flourish and to see God glorified in all that we do.

1

TAKING DOMINION AND THE PROBLEM WITH GOOD AND EVIL

Taking dominion God's way

According to the beginning of the Bible, in the first two chapters of Genesis, humans were created to be relational beings. We were created to be like God. This likeness was not in omniscience, knowing everything, or in omnipresence, being everywhere, or omnipotence having power over everything. Rather it was the likeness of other qualities of God, and in particular, in connection to the topic of this book, relational likeness. We were made to relate to Him, to each other and to the world in which we were placed.

Then God said, "Let us make man in our image, in our likeness, and let them rule over the fish of the sea and the birds of the air, over livestock, over all the earth, and over the creatures that move along the ground" (Genesis 1:26).

The Hebrew word for God in this chapter is *Elohim*. It was a plural word meaning something like "The most holy (or other) ones". Notice the words 'us' and 'our' in this verse. God was presenting Himself (or Themselves) as a perfect community in unity, serving one another to do what He had called them to do. Thus, it is implied that humans were to be like God, living in relationship to God His creation and each other, serving one another as they went about the work at hand. He gave them the skills of language and strategic thinking so that they were able to plan and work together in this calling. God gave them a measure of the ability to think like Him, create things like Him, and relate together like Him. Just as He saw His creation was "good" or "very good", humans were to admire and value His creation, and with this attitude rule over it. God, as the creator and sustainer of everything, is the sovereign ruler of everything. His Word, His law controls the very fabric of all that is. He gave humans, created in His image, the capacity and will to take dominion. With constant communication, listening to the voice of God, we can have the wisdom, the knowledge of what to do, to take dominion. This dominion was to be applied to the created order on earth and was to have expression in all the various specific spheres of activity to which He calls us.

The biblical story transitions its focus from the creation of heaven and earth to the relationship of God to the humans. The name used for God now is the LORD, Yahweh in the Hebrew. This is the name of God used through much of the ongoing biblical story. It focuses on God's eternal and supreme authority or sovereignty. Just as God was Sovereign Lord of everything He created, so humans were to work with Him, ruling over (taking dominion or managing) God's creation on earth. But man was not to be Sovereign Lord. Rather, God told humans what to do. Humans were to listen to and obey God's instructions, God's law. It was God who was to be the king of the developing human community. They in turn were to be kings of, or rule over their environment. God was king, governor, emperor, master, Lord over all humans. Humans were like 'ministers of the crown', representing Him and accountable to Him.

When God was about to create the second human He said, "It is not good for the human to be alone. I will make a helper suitable for him." Then the story describes the man embarking on his work under the leadership of the LORD God. This involved observing and naming the great variety of living things. Then the LORD created 'the suitable helper'. God created humans to help each other to fulfil their calling. Marriage and all social relationships to follow were to be structured for the purpose of serving the king's purpose for them, of multiplying and managing the living things and their environment, to the glory of God.

Adam realised that, unlike the animals he was observing and managing, she was just like him. The man said, "This is now bone of my bones and flesh of my flesh, she shall be called 'woman' for she was taken out of man." The initial use of the word translated 'woman' was clearly meant to mean 'another human'. Together they would share the responsibility of their calling as humans, the rulership or management of the creation on the earth. They lived in daily intimate relationship to God and each other, transparently working together without any hidden selfish agendas but just setting out to fulfil God's purpose for them. They "were both naked and felt no shame." This was the initial kingdom of heaven on earth, complete obedience to the king of heaven – God's will "on earth as it is in heaven".

The social consequences of sin

The story of the fall in Genesis chapter 3 inaugurates the beginning of a pattern of human relationships, of how broken people are inclined to relate. God said,

> But you must not eat from the tree of the knowledge of good and evil, for when you eat from it you shall surely die. (Genesis 2:17)

Satan said,

> For God knows that when you eat from it your eyes will be opened, and you will be like God, knowing good and evil. (Genesis 3:5)

At the core of sin is the desire to decide for ourselves what is right and wrong, what is good and what is evil, wanting to be like God, deciding for ourselves what we ought or ought not to do, what is good and what is evil. They rejected God's leadership. As far as they were concerned God was no longer the king of their lives. They, rather than God, were calling the shots. They wanted to 'do it their way', or 'be a law to themselves'. They were tempted to "be like God" in this regard, to be ultimately sovereign. But in reality, they chose to conduct their lives, not in the image of God, but rather in the image of Satan, in rebellion. This is the image of God living a self-destructive lie, defying the sovereignty of God.

The first result of their sin was that gripping sense of guilt and shame, and they felt a need to hide from each other and from God to whom they were accountable. Communication breakdown and broken relationships are a fundamental result of sin, and a root cause of further sins.

Next, the story relates their attempt to avoid responsibility for their error and deflect the blame. It's the fault of "the other human you put here with me". This dishonest self-examination, this inclination of blame shifting has permeated human relationships ever since. "It's my brother's fault" syndrome gets applied in various ways and, as we shall note through this book, it becomes: 'It's the fault of the system for which the government is responsible'. We easily slip into the attitude of refusing to recognise that we are part of the problem and hence fail to see that we should be part of the solution. Rather, we tend to think it is the other's fault and their responsibility to fix it.

Next, God declares the consequences of human sin. They include a broken relationship with creation, including difficulties and pain in fulfilling the calling to multiply and to manage the earth. And then he describes a broken relationship with each other. Then, He points out to the woman the nature of their now flawed social relationships.

As a result of sin, to the woman he said,

> "...Your desire will be for your husband, and he will rule over you." (Genesis 3:16)

And to the man he said,

"Because you listened to [obeyed] your wife..." (Genesis 3:17)

They both disobeyed God and listened to other voices. Having rejected the rulership of God, humans (in this case, the woman) would now seek to be led by a fellow human (in this case, the man). Scholars say that this word "desire" has the sense of seeking out by moving low to the ground, and it can be applied to the marriage context, or to an animal of prey seeking out food, or to seeking the comfort of another's leadership. As fallen humans we have an urge to seek out and to worship something or someone other than God. This desire to seek out and even idolise another, rather than God to lead us, is a direct and immediate result of sin.

In response, those who realise they are being 'sought after' will opportunistically rule over or dominate those who desire their leadership. This description of human relationships is not the way it was originally designed to be. It is a direct result of sin. We were made to seek out and worship God our leader, our king. He, not another human, was to be in command and control. This disposition to rule over others is the beginning of a lust for power, which is seen in the ongoing history of human society. And herein is the seed of the human disposition to abuse power, often referred to in conjunction with the expression 'power corrupts'.

It is a result of sin that human rulership over other humans is needed, and, as we will explain later in this book, the degree of authority (command and control) is in proportion to the degree of failure of people to submit to the authority of God.

It was not until this point in the biblical story that Adam gives the other human her own name, Eve. They were no longer identified by each other by their relationship to each other. Rather, they each now had their own name, Adam and Eve. Maybe this can be seen as the embryonic beginning of rampant individualism?

It is at this point that they were denied access to the Tree of Life. It has been suggested that the Tree of Life is a reference to the Spirit of Life, the Holy Spirit. See, for example, Romans chapter 8, which speaks of the law of sin and death verses the law of the Spirit of Life. With the sustaining and empowering of the Holy Spirit withdrawn from them, they were subject to corruption and death.

Sin taking dominion

The story of Cain and Abel in Genesis 4 begins with them realising their broken relationship with God, and so they attempt to appease Him with offerings. Here is the beginning of religion, attempting to restore relationship with God through our effort. The LORD looked on Abel's offering with favour, but on Cain's unfavourably. Cain was angry about this. What God had to say to Cain about this reveals why his offering was unacceptable. It was not necessarily the substance being offered (although we do see Abel's offering as a type of the coming sacrificial lamb), but rather it was Cain's attitude of heart. Abel had an attitude of faith, Cain of fear or resentment.

Cain sought to relate to God, but to do it his way. And at the same time, he did not resist the temptation to have a negative attitude toward his brother. The Lord said to Cain:

"...if you do not do what is right, sin is crouching at your door, it desires to have you, but you must rule over it." (Genesis 4:7)

This introduces us to the principle that if we do not overcome the temptation to sin, sin will overcome us (see Romans chapter 6). Self-control or self-government in the sense of ruling over temptation to sin is a key to ongoing fellowship with God and our fellow-humans. This is a significant factor in the outworking of government, as I explain later. Augustine of Hippo said in City of God that he who becomes protector of sin shall surely become its prisoner.

Cain worked out this attitude by murdering his brother. By hatred and murder, he despised the image of God in his brother. When confronted by God, Cain said, "...Am I my brother's keeper?" Effectively he was saying, "Why should I care about the welfare of others! I will look after number one, thank you very much!" This attitude is the root cause of social chaos, the foundation of violent anarchy, and the antithesis of the objective of good government.

Cain perceived that Abel had a more acceptable relationship to God. He resented this and failed to resist the temptation to kill him. The urge to control or eliminate the person who is perceived to have a superior relationship with God is at the heart of religious violence and war. Anti-religion or bad religion is inevitably involved in the cause and/or the justification of the violence of war. Violence is rooted in the heart of the perpetrator, not in the difference of religious practice.

Taking dominion another way – to cope with the curse

The Lord said to Cain:

> "Now you are under a curse and driven from the ground …When you work the ground, it will no longer yield its crops for you. You will be a restless wanderer on the earth." (Genesis 4:11-12)

And Cain responded:

> "My punishment is more than I can bear. Today you are driving me from the land, and I will be hidden from your presence; I will be a restless wanderer on the earth, and whoever finds me will kill me." (Genesis 4:13-14)

Cain had become disconnected from the LORD, from his family, and from the productive land. This curse was overwhelming. He was desperate to belong to something secure and greater than himself, and to belong to or be connected to the land. And so, the story goes on to tell how he initiated his substitute for God and for Eden, and a way to protect himself from those who may seek revenge for the death of Abel. He built a city.

This Hebrew word for city implies far more than the gathering of people dwelling in a confined area. It has embedded in it the sense of a watching angel or a vengeful spirit that is behind the city. The city comes with political and spiritual power. The city becomes an object of worship. Many ancient cities were synonymous with a god or goddess. In place of the LORD, the city becomes the essence of community purpose. The people rally together to boost the prestige of the city. Citizenship becomes the essence of people's identity. The city is an embryonic nation/state and thus this is the beginning of self-absorbed nationalism.

City-building would become the socio-political pattern of humans banished from Eden. It is characterised by separation from God, frustration in earth management, scarcity of and competition for resources, wandering, and vengeance toward others who would oppose them.

Rejecting the legitimate king of the world, humans, in defiance of the legitimate government of God, developed tribes, effectively family 'gangs'. Cain's family initiated the rise of the city state, with the naming and leadership being organised along family lines. Thus, this is the beginning of the pattern of family dynasties, the fear of other tribal groups and the need to promote and defend the local socio-political community. See the latter part of Genesis 4.

The trinitarian God is the original ordered community, the three persons of the Trinity working together for their common good. Created in His image, we are made to represent this order in our community life, as we fulfil our calling to take dominion on the earth. Thinkers have at times said that we are 'social animals', wanting to organise our community lives to achieve some greater good. Without connection to God, this inevitably turns out to be greater evil.

The Bible's description of society leading up to the flood is a continuation of the story of Cain, followed through in all families. It is all about unbridled self-indulgence and disrespect for others created in the image of God.

> The LORD saw how great the wickedness of the human race had become on the earth, and that every inclination of the thoughts of the human heart was only evil all the time. (Genesis 6:5)

> Now the earth was corrupt in God's sight and was full of violence. (Genesis 6:11)

Human sin, centred on independence from the rulership of God, has derailed the use of our capacity to take dominion over creation. It is the fall that has led to the desire and need for human rulership over others. The city is not the cause of the problem, but it is what God led humans to do as they attempted to control or reduce the cursed effects of sin. It is the sin in humans that has developed the lust for power. Our sin has led to social conflict, violence, war and chaos.

The need for accountability

Recently I found myself in conversation with a friend about climate change and governments' responses to it. I found myself saying that even though I had been a science teacher, I did not think I had the right to be opinionated about the issue. However, I said climate change is not a new phenomenon – it appears that 'Noah's flood', recorded in Genesis 6 to 8, was a major climate change event. We don't think it was caused by the burning of fossil fuels, but it was a consequence of really bad human behaviour that demanded consequences and further human governmental control.

God had already pronounced reduced expected life span as a result of sin (Genesis 6:3). But further mitigation of the effect of sin was needed. There needed to be accountability for sin, their unrighteousness. Hence God chose to eliminate the people by flood. Noah and his family alone were exempt from this judgment, per virtue of Noah's righteousness, which was intrinsically linked to his relationship with God.

> Noah was a righteous man, blameless among the people of his time, and he walked faithfully with God. (Genesis 6:9)

> Noah did everything just as God commanded him. (Genesis 6:22)

After the flood God recommissioned Noah and his sons to rule over the animals, to carefully use them to meet their need for resources. In the process they were to be accountable, firstly to God. And then, in relationship to human life, He said:

> ...and from each human being, too, I will demand an accounting for the life of another human being. Whoever

sheds human blood, by humans shall their blood be shed: for in the image of God has God made mankind. (Genesis 9:5,6)

Herein lies the beginnings of an understanding of the need for accountability in this life, to mitigate the effects of sin. The value of human life rooted in an understanding that we are made in God's image should be a fundamental value underpinning social and political relationships.

This sense of accountability is worked out in various ways in diverse cultures. In many cultures there is the concept of correcting social injustice by returning like for like, "an eye for an eye". This is often seen as a social responsibility, not just as selfish revenge. In New Zealand where I live, the Māori concept referred to as 'utu', I am told, has this sense of restoring just balance. Similarly, in Australia the aboriginal concept of 'makarrata' involves restoration (or payback) to bring about restitution or reconciliation. In some pantheistic cultures, this social justice is linked to a spiritual inevitability called 'karma', and the correction of social justice and injustice will be worked out through reincarnation in the next life. This has contributed to the intrenchment of inviolable 'caste' systems. The elevation of lower caste persons is seen as violating karma. In each culture there is this sense of social accountability.

As we will describe further in this book, in societies influenced by biblical revelation, this accountability is worked out through legal systems based on God's law. Hence many see in Genesis 9 the signalling of the need for civil government and justice systems.

The rise of kingdoms and imperialism

The biblical narrative in Genesis 10 outlines the ensuing descendants of the sons of Noah. The socio-political features of this account include:

- Patriarchal families and tribes.
- Domination by hunter warriors.
- Occupation of territories.
- Various languages.

These features would characterise the political organisation of the world. There would be tribal chiefs or kings who were much like successful gang leaders. And there would be nepotism, the handing on of power along family lines. Although these kings' motivation was most likely sinful, God ordained it to be this way.

In the table of the families of the sons of Noah in Genesis 10, a little more detail is given to the life of Nimrod, a grandson of the cursed Ham.

> Nimrod... became a mighty warrior. He was a mighty hunter before the Lord... The first centers of his kingdom were Babylon, Uruk, Akkad and Kalneh, in Shinar. From that land he went to Assyria, where he built Nineveh, Reboth Ir, Calah and Resen... (Genesis 10:8-12)

This city-builder began the phenomenon of rulership over multiple cities. He was the first empire builder. Under the observation of the Lord, this hunter-warrior used his vengeful plundering ways to subdue and control others. The spirit of the city becomes the seat of piracy, terrorism, war and empire building.

Genesis 11 focuses on the first of Nimrod's cities, Babylon. The story of the Tower of Babel describes the intent to develop political power and prestige – selfish sovereignty as opposed to the sovereignty of God.

> Then they said, "Come let us build ourselves a city, with a tower that reaches to the heavens, so that we may make a name for ourselves…" (Genesis 11:4)

The expression "make a name for ourselves" implies more than building prestige. It means choosing for themselves a name independent of the name that God gives them. They chose their own identity and notoriety. Rather than being made in the image of God, they wanted to choose their own identity.

With their disposition for political power and prestige, their motivation to be like God, the people concentrated their society around a structure which symbolised their corporate wish to be proudly in control of their own lives. With God pushed out of the picture, they were determined that their will, their culture, and their political power would dominate the whole of human society. They were desiring to usurp God's role as sovereign king. They strove to bring all glory to themselves.

This tower was a representation of the spirit of one world human government or control, a theme continued in biblical prophecy under the name of 'Babylon'. The confusion of languages was God's way of frustrating this drive to concentrate all power and prestige in one human society. This God-rejecting and human-glorifying motivation was still possessing their hearts, but it would now be worked out in many diverse and competing kingdoms. This was the beginning of separate nations formed on the basis of shared language. The Tower of Babel story shows diverse nations were God's idea. God's intervention was the origin of language difference and diverse people groups.

> From one man He made all the nations, that they should inhabit the whole earth; and he marked out their appointed times in history and the boundaries of their lands... (Acts 17:26)

Thus, the nature of the political structures of the world was developing. Patriarchs would exercise power over their extended families. These groups developed into territorial tribes. Each people group was led by a strongman, a chief. The 'establishment' was much like competing gangs who were loyal to their gang leader. Successful gang leaders rallied their warrior/supporters around them. If a chief could achieve the support of and control of more than their own gang, they would be formally recognised as 'king'.

One thing we learn from stories of the life of gangs and their leaders, is that successful leaders intuitively live by some sort of code of ethics. It is a self-made set of morals. It invariably involves loyalty to the leader and the group, and it has values antagonistic to God's ethics. For example, the value of human life is likely to be low, with disrespect for the life and wellbeing of people other than the group. Values are more likely to be some type of honour and shame or prestige and power. A strict ethic of loyalty often predominates. The gang headquarters are much like their fortified city. The police are seen as the enforcers of the main opposing gang. This is much like the way the politics of the ancient world developed. Augustine of Hippo said in City of God that kingdoms without justice are just gangs of bandits.

The Hebrew word for king or kingship, *melek*, appears to be connected to the idea of possession. The king would possess (or own) subjects and territory. With the expansion of and control of more people groups, kingdoms became in time empires, ruled by a monarch which we have come to call an emperor.

Often the king's authority would be fortified or justified by the idea that he represented or was specially connected to a god. In some cases he was considered a god himself. Thus developed the concept of 'the divine right of kings' to exercise undisputed command and control.

This tribal power and conflict is all an outworking of the spirit of Adam, Cain, Nimrod and the tribes of men and their leaders spoken of in Genesis. How quickly our sinful inclinations drag us away from living peacefully under the sovereignty of God!

REFLECTIONS

Considering our social activity, our work in the public square:

God has called us all and given us all a capacity to 'take dominion'. We work this out in a wide range of callings. For example, artisans will take dominion over materials and shape them to fulfil the vision of what they have in mind to create. We may find ourselves managing finances, building design, attending to people's health, the welfare of family and children, or a range of other specific callings. These may be in the context of commercial, service or voluntary organisations, sporting groups, church organisations, political organisations or in any number of other 'spheres of influence'.

The *why* questions:

What is my/our purpose?

How is God involved in my/our purpose?

How is the vision or mission of our organisation in keeping with the purposes of God?

Is the bottom line to make money, gain power or fame? Or is the bottom line the good (or flourishing) of people?

Is the bottom line to the glory of God?

The *how* questions:

How do we decide what to do? Whom do we consult?

How is doing it 'my way,' operating in the mode of Adam and Cain?

How are we submitted to the higher authority of God?

How do we daily position ourselves in communication with Him? How are we listening to His voice and obeying Him?

How are we doing it in right relationship to others?

In what way do we regard others as created in the image of God?

How do we respect and honour their potential to work in relationship with and in the likeness of God? What does this look like in practice?

The *what now* questions:

What do I (or we) need to do to correct or improve our way of taking dominion?

How am I going to make these changes in keeping with the purposes and principles of God?

2

THE PURPOSE OF A GOD-FEARING NATION

The call of a nation

It was in the context of social violence and 'Nimrodian' cities that God chose to separate out one patriarch and his family to be the channel of His blessing, His salvation, His restoration of the people of the world. God chose Abram, a resident of a city in the region where Nimrod had established cities. He was chosen, not because of his political leadership and prowess, nor his ability as a warrior lord. Rather, Abram was chosen because of his disposition to listen to, trust and obey God. Abraham addressed God as Sovereign Lord, and he listened to what God said.

> Abram believed the LORD, and He credited it to him as righteousness. (Genesis 15:6)

God declared to Abram the purpose of his family-nation:

"I will make you into a great nation,
And I will bless you;
I will make your name great,
And you will be a blessing.
I will bless those who bless you,
And whoever curses you I will curse;
And all the peoples on earth
Will be blessed through you." (Genesis 12:2,3)

Abram's family-nation would be different in nature to all other nations. It was not to be a self-centred, self-consuming nation like those developing in the world of his time. The central difference would be its core spirit. It would not be centred around a king and a city. Its focal point would be God. It was not to be making a name for itself like Babylon. Rather it would be declaring the name of the LORD! The LORD would give the nation meaning, belonging and purpose. The LORD was to be the motivator and guide to all its actions.

The nation would be great, not necessarily in size, but in flourishing and exemplary influence. The word, 'a blessing' could be translated as 'seen as blessed'. The nation was envisaged by God to be an example of flourishing and a channel of blessing.

"...you will be for me a kingdom of priests and a holy nation." (Exodus 19:5)

This nation, Israel, was to be a nation of priests. A priest is a mediator between God and the rest of the people. The word holy means set apart, totally other or different, as God is totally set apart and different to humans and gods conceived by humans. The nation's purpose was to reflect to the world who God is and what God is like. They were to be a representation of His holiness for the world to see.

Israel was to be the 'classroom' in which God revealed Himself and His plan of salvation to the world. The political organisation of Israel, as described in chapter 3, is part of this God-orchestrated learning process.

Nationhood and nationalism can be an instrument for good when the nation's purpose is to inform the world what God is like and what God has to say to the world. Such an outward-looking nation can thrive so that others beyond its borders can also flourish. People who hate such nations, and/or terrorise them, will be subject to the wrath of God, as God said to Abraham: "Whoever curses you I will curse" (Genesis 12:3).

Conversely, if a nation seeks to be great in that it is self-promoting at the expense of others, it will not be 'blessed'. If a nation seeks to be economically superior and prestigious to the effect of putting other nations down, it will be economically and socially a curse, not a blessing. If it seeks political power over others and becomes imperialistic in spirit and practice, other nations will seek to resist it and destroy it. This type of nationalism, fascism or imperialism is portrayed in prophetic scripture as 'Babylon'. Typically, the leaders of such nations don't have a sense of accountability to God, and they are or become authoritarian or dictatorial. They sometimes try to hide this independence of God by wooing the support of religion or the church. This promotion of self and the nation in place of God is of the spirit of 'anti-Christ', as expressed by the apostle John in his epistles and the book of Revelation.

This form of nationalism is invariably captive to this authoritarian leader, who not only reinforces his own power but oppresses or eliminates any opposition. Nations displaying this centralisation of power and the promotion of the nation at the expense of others have existed in the world in all generations since the beginning of the rise of city nations.

When Abraham's grandson Jacob returned to the land which God had called Abraham, God reaffirmed the call to Abraham with him.

> "Your name will no longer be Jacob, but Israel, because you have struggled with God and with humans and have overcome." (Genesis 32:28)

Clearly, he and the nation descended from him were not to make a name for themselves as other nations did. They were to take on the name God gave them. The name Israel means 'rules with or as God' or 'God prevails', reminding them that they were to continue to take dominion in a dynamic (wrestling) relationship with Him.

> And God said to Israel, "I am God Almighty; be fruitful and increase in number. A nation and a community of nations will come from you, and kings will be among your descendants. The land I gave to Abraham and Isaac I also give to you, and I will give this land to your descendants after you." (Genesis 35:11-12)

Israel was to be different from the nations around them, from the pattern of this world. Connection with Him, with each other and with the land was to be the core nature of the nation. The nation was to be blessed as it was to be a blessing beyond its borders. This was the nation's responsibility.

Jesus said:

"From everyone who has been given much, much will be demanded; and from the one who has been entrusted much, much more will be asked." (Luke 12:48)

We who have been blessed are obligated to be a blessing.

A Godly political leader

The latter part of the book of Genesis relates the story of Joseph, who exemplifies the blessing of God extended to others. Joseph had a dream in which all of his family bowed before him as their leader. This mirrors what God said Eve would do, desire the leadership of and bow to Adam. His brothers could not cope with the idea of their younger brother, their father's favourite, exercising dominion over them and so they put him into the custody of slave traders. Joseph's journey took him from slavery and imprisonment to political leadership directly under the king of Egypt. He gained this position because of his integrity and God-given wisdom. We read repeatedly that God was with Joseph. He resisted temptation because he did not want to sin against God.

> The LORD was with Joseph so that he prospered... (Genesis 39:2)
>
> From the time he put him in charge of his household and of all that he owned, the LORD blessed the household of the Egyptian because of Joseph. The blessing of the LORD was on everything Potiphar had, both in the house and in the field. (Genesis 39:5)

Regular connection with God results in the blessing of flourishing. Clearly, Joseph was consciously with God. His relationship with God was at the base of all his decisions. When Potiphar's wife attempted to seduce him, he responded by saying he would not break his master's trust and "How then could I do such a wicked thing and sin against God?" (Genesis 39:9).

A key to his character development and gaining positions of responsibility was his daily relationship with God. He respected and honoured God. He listened to God, who gave him the interpretation of dreams. Joseph understood the time in which Egypt was living. And God gave him insight into what to do, a strategic plan for the economy of the nation, to provide for the good of all the people of Egypt.

He understood it was God's calling on his life. He made it clear to his brothers that:

> "...God sent me ahead of you to preserve for you a remnant on earth and to save your lives by a great deliverance." [and] "God has made me lord of all Egypt." (See Genesis 45:5-10)

Joseph was a prime minister living as a servant leader, working for the common good of the people. Joseph did not succumb to the lust for power and prestige prevalent in the political leadership in the world. We see Joseph, in this respect, as a foreshadowing type of Christ the King, who would humble Himself, submit to the will of God and sacrificially serve for the good of all.

Joseph makes a wonderful model for anyone who is called to be involved in leadership and, in particular, in government.

REFLECTIONS

Thinking about Abram/Abraham:

Read Ephesians 1 together.

In Christ, we are all called to be children of Abraham – blessed and thus to be a blessing.

Do you see yourself as 'blessed'? In what ways has this blessing worked out in your life?

How do you remind yourself that I am blessed to be a blessing?

How does this look like in the church, the family, the organisation, or business in which you work?

How can a church bless other people and other churches, rather than compete with them?

In what way could we expect our nation to have this sort of attitude toward others?

Thinking about Joseph:

We all influence and thereby lead others. If you are in a position of leadership – unofficially or officially recognised, ask yourself:

What can I learn from Joseph and apply to my personal life?

How do I lead by example? What message is my example giving?

How do I lead by serving others?

How do I lead by inspiring and enabling those whom I lead? How can I overcome the tendency to always command and control?

Do I get those whom I lead to do it my way, micro-manage, or do I share and inspire in the vision for the organisation and then enable those whom I lead to do it in the way God has shaped them to do it?

How do I enable those whom I lead to position themselves to listen to God as they do their role?

Thinking about current political leadership:

It is prudent for those in political leadership to examine their personal and national purpose and practice, asking the question, "What type of nation are we seeking to promote?"

It is prudent for political supporters to ask themselves: "Are we backing the right sort of nationhood? Are we seeking the good of all nations or our own imperial power? Are we wanting our nation to be self-consuming or positively outward-looking?"

3

THE RULE OF GOD THROUGH THE RULE OF LAW

Israel's king is ... The LORD

There was divine purpose behind the miraculous events of the exodus of the people of Israel out of Egypt. God was making the point that He, not Moses or anyone else, was their deliverer. After the deliverance of the nation from the Egyptian armies at the Red Sea, Moses and his sister Miriam sing a song reflecting on the event. It is recorded in Exodus 15. It begins:

> "I will sing to the LORD, for He is highly exalted... The LORD is my strength and my defence; He has become my salvation. He is my God, and I will praise Him... The LORD is a warrior, the LORD is His name..."

The Exodus story continues to express how these events reveal that He is sovereign king, warrior, deliverer, "majestic in holiness, awesome in glory..." and it ends with, "The LORD will reign for ever and ever."

God was establishing in the consciousness of the people that *He* is their king. As they journeyed on, in the next part of the story, God revealed Himself as their healer, their provider, their banner, their deliverer, their mission-giver. *He* was their heroic leader to be celebrated, to be praised, and to be faithfully followed and obeyed. Israel was to be a theocracy (ruled by God).

Representative rulers

Then the narrative comes to the story of Moses attempting to be the arbitrator (judge) to resolve all disputes amongst the people. With the advice of Jethro and the guidance of the Lord, men who feared God and lived for the good of the people and not personal gain were chosen to be judges over various groups of the people. Their character was to be consistent with the spirit of the law – God honouring, not self-promoting. They were to be thoroughly familiar with the details of the law, and how to administer it. They were not law makers, but law administers. They were to effectively rule, in the sense of arbitrate, over the people they represented.

God did not want Moses to take on the role of a national king. God was king. Indeed, the spread of political power was characteristic of the organisation of the administration of the civil law in the nation about to be set up. Thus, this arrangement is the forerunner of the idea of law courts and representative government.

Israel as intermediary

At the mountain of Sinai, God would give the detailed law code by which the nation of Israel was to live. This was to be the political structure and ethics by which the whole nation was to be governed. God was to educate them on what He determined was good and evil, right and wrong. Before spelling out the substance of the Law, God explained the significance of the nation and this law.

> "...now if you obey me fully and keep my covenant, then out of all nations you will be my treasured possession. Although the whole earth is mine, you will be for me a kingdom of priests and a holy nation." (Exodus 19:5)

The nation of Israel was designed to be an intermediary between God and the world. As promised to Abraham, the nation was to be blessed to be a blessing. God had graciously saved them from slavery and oppression and was now commissioning them. Following His law was the means, not of their salvation, but of their role in God's mission. Israel would be the messenger to the world of His revelation of what is the core problem in the world, of what is right and wrong, and of the need for God's salvation. Being an intermediary necessitates thoroughly knowing God and His ways and demonstrating that relationship in all of life.

This covenantal arrangement was a step in God's ultimate plan for the whole world. It included the political structure as an example of how it should be. There were three components of government: legislation, administration, and arbitration.

Legislation

Moses introduced theocracy (the rule of God) through the rule of law. God through Moses was the legislator.

The Hebrew name for this law is 'Torah'. Its meaning is far broader than the English word 'law', as in criminal law. It could be translated as 'instruction' or 'guide to the good life'. Unlike other ancient law codes, it was far more comprehensive with over 600 laws to guide all aspects of life. It does include hard and fast imperatives (e.g. "You shall not......") with the corresponding imposed consequences, but it has more. It includes personal and community morality, such as how to relate to foreigners, and to care for widows and the poor, and how to conduct economic life with integrity. It also includes guidelines for ceremonial rituals and life patterns, such as the calendar of holy days, and the description of sacrifices. In other ancient nations, ethical behaviour was not interconnected with religious worship of gods, because their gods were not holy ethical beings. Three categories of legislation – the legal, the moral, and the ceremonial are at times considered as three separate types of law. But often they are presented in an integrated way. The whole gist of the Torah is that all of life is to be lived in relationship with the LORD. The net result of this way of living is the flourishing of all the people of the nation, the common wealth or 'shalom', the blessing as promised to Abraham.

The outline of this legislation begins with the Ten Commandments, which encapsulate in legal terms the priorities and values God's people should have. The first four of these are:

- the exclusive Lordship of God as king and ruler over every aspect of life,
- the need to resist living with other objects or purposes instead of Him,
- the protection of the reputation and glory of God, and
- the need to work and rest, focusing on connection with God.

Thus, the first four of the ten commandments outline that their relationship to God was to be the focus and an integral part of every aspect of their lives.

Then the ensuing commandments summarise how this God-centredness was to be worked out in social relationships with immediate family and community. These prior values were:

- the value of respect, especially the priority of family, in social relationships,
- the prior value of all human life,
- the value of marriage as a committed covenantal relationship,
- the value of respecting others' property rights,
- the value of truth, honesty, and
- the value of desiring God, rather than that which others have.

These commandments are foundational expressions of human rights and responsibilities. Wouldn't it be refreshing, in our contemporary world, if a political party would express these priorities as the foundation of their legislative priorities and practice?

The 'law of Moses' was comprehensive in shaping virtually every aspect of their lives. For example, the statutes immediately following the Ten Commandments involve laws related to employment, injury causing violence, property, social relations, social justice, and holy days. Much of the rest of Exodus relates to the design and use of the tent of meeting, the 'tabernacle' of God. The next book, Leviticus, as its name suggests, spells out the role and oversight responsibilities of the Levitical priesthood. It includes many rules governing a wide range of aspects of community life. Then Numbers continues the story of the nation's travels and their preparation to enter the 'promised land'. It relates the story of the counting of the population before and after the 40 years of wandering in the desert. This wandering was because they failed to trust God as their deliverer and king. Finally, Deuteronomy is a second statement of the law with particular emphasis on things related to the occupation of the land.

It is a massive study to look at these various laws and discern the principles behind them. It is not the purpose of this book to outline the detail of over 600 laws spelled out in the Torah, but rather to highlight the political structures and processes that God instituted.

However, it is a valuable exercise to discern God's principles on an issue by researching the laws related to it. For example, the law about infectious diseases is an apt topic in the 2020s. When Israel was about to receive the Law, God said:

> If you diligently listen to the voice of the Lord... I will put none of these diseases which I have brought upon the Egyptians, for I am the Lord that heals you. (Exodus 15:26)

Leviticus 13-15 are the chapters dealing with what to do about skin infections. Remember, these instructions were given thousands of years before there was an understanding of what we call microbiology. The passage begins with "The LORD said to Moses and Aaron..." Moses and Aaron did not have much if any understanding of how infectious diseases were transmitted. They were merely the messengers. The people of Israel did not know the scientific laws of God to live by, but they had God's special revelation to them, the Law of Moses, to heed and obey. All their actions were to be done in the context of their obedient relationship to God.

So what were they to do about infections? Here is a summary:

- They were to be observant. They were to look out for swellings, rashes, spots, sores and discharges.
- They were to take themselves to the professionals (the priests in Israel were the health professionals) to be tested, to be diagnosed.
- Before diagnosis, the symptomatic person was to be regarded as infectious (*unclean*).

- If the diagnosis was positive, they were to be isolated for seven days and then to be retested.
- If they were found to be disease free, they were declared clean.
- Any points of contact such as clothing and skin of the infected person were to be washed thoroughly, before they could be declared clean again.
- An infected person was to make it very clear that they were 'unclean' and were to practice isolation or physical distancing.
- After being declared clean again, they were to make a special offering in the tabernacle or temple. (This was effectively paying the priest, the doctor, for his services.)
- Regular washing, especially before meals was to be practised by all.

If the people of Israel were familiar with and obeyed these laws, they would bless their neighbour and be an example to the observing world of the blessings of living in relationship with their Creator and Lord.

Administration

Each family and local community was to live in relationship with God by teaching the law to the next generation, and then administering the law.

The responsibility to fulfil the law rested on every individual, every family, and every local community. When the land was apportioned to the people, the tribe of Levi did not own any farmland, but rather were living in each local community. The Levites were effectively the public service, ensuring that the law was taught and enacted. As the name 'priest' means, they were the mediators between God, the legislator, and the people. They were paid from the tithes (equivalent of taxes) and offerings (equivalent of administrative fees) of the people. They were the medical professionals, diagnosing, for example, infectious diseases. They were the experts in the law, helping families educate the next generation in the details of the law that they were responsible to maintain.

Arbitration/judiciary

Following the pattern set by Moses and Jethro before the law was given, there were to be local judges to call upon to adjudicate difficult cases.

> At that time, I [Moses] said to you: You are too heavy a burden for me to carry alone... How can I bear your problems and your burdens and your disputes all by myself? Choose some wise, understanding and respected men from each of your tribes, and I will set them over you... So I took the leading men of your tribes, wise and respected men, and appointed them to have authority over you – as commanders of thousands, of hundreds, of fifties and of tens and as tribal officials. And I charged your judges at that time, "Here the disputes between your people and judge fairly, whether the

case is between two Israelites or between an Israelite and a foreigner residing among you. Do not show partiality in judging; hear both small and great alike. Do not be afraid of anyone, for judgement belongs to God... (Deuteronomy 1:9-18)

Choose some wise, understanding and respected men:
These judges were to be characterised by wisdom, understanding and respect. Character, not political or military power, is an essential qualification for good government that enables the flourishing of all the people. The judges' attitude towards God would determine their wisdom and understanding necessary for them to represent God.

The people themselves were to choose them:
Herein is a pattern of representative government, a pattern adopted by nations many hundreds of years later. This was in the thinking of the protestant reformers, such as John Knox, who worked through the idea of the priesthood of all believers into the concept of modern free nations where the people chose their representatives to govern them.

Judge fairly, whether the case is between two Israelites or between an Israelite and a foreigner residing among you:
This was not an invitation to revise God's legislation to accommodate the ungodly attitudes and values of foreign peoples. This was an instruction to the judiciary. This was guidance to avoid xenophobic or racially biased prejudices affecting their judgement. Foreigners would most likely be ignorant of God's

law of the land, but this was not an excuse to exempt some of the people living in the land from following the law of the land.

Do not show partiality in judging; hear both small and great alike:
All people stood equally before God's holy law. Economic power, or the ability to bribe or pay for their sin was not to be a factor in their judgement.

Do not be afraid of anyone, for judgement belongs to God:
It was the LORD their King who was to be feared. The judges were agents of the Holy LORD. The people stood before, not the judge, but the LORD as their authoritative king.

As Israel became established in the land, these judges would come to be based in each town. They would sit together in a place at the town 'gate' to consult, to deliberate and decide what to do. These elders were to be thoroughly familiar with God and with the details of the law so that they could arbitrate fairly. For more detail, see Deuteronomy 16:18-20, 22:15 and 25:7 and Proverbs 31:2-3.

It seems that when there was a time of trouble, God would raise up someone, often a local judge, to organise the military defence of the community. If that person were to listen to God, God would bring about the victory. The book of Judges tells stories of how this worked out in practice during the following 200 or so years.

The ultimate purpose

At this point it needs to be noted that the prime purpose of the law was not to effect deliverance or salvation but to orientate the people toward God who desired to bless them, and to prepare the people for and lead them to the Deliverer, the Saviour, who was God Himself. This will be spelled out when we get to looking at the New Testament teaching about the law.

Unlike most other nations or people groups, there was no nationally organised king to tell individuals what to do or not do. There was no king exercising command and control. That was God's role. The people were to conduct their lives under the control of the Sovereign Lord.

The kings of some ancient nations were considered gods, or the king was understood to be the living image of a god. They were to be worshipped and obeyed, like the relationship of the fallen Adam and Eve. But Israel was to understand that all people are created in the image of God and all have the privilege and responsibility to reflect the righteousness of God. As mentioned before, this arrangement is the ideological foundation of the modern Christian 'democracy'. This will be discussed later in this book.

The challenge: a blessing or a curse

In Israel there was to be theocratic legislation and local administration of the rule of law. Everyone in a position of authority, whether that be in the sphere of the family, educational, economic, governing servant/employees or civil community was to be directly subject to the authority of God. It was dependent on all the people, not just the leaders, rising to the responsibility of living in obedient relationship to the Lord who was their king.

> "...the word is very near you; it is in your mouth and in your heart so you may obey it. See, I set before you today life and prosperity, death and destruction. For I command you today to love the LORD your God, to walk in obedience to Him, and to keep His commands, decrees and laws; then you will live and increase, and the LORD your God will bless you in the land you are entering to possess. But if your heart turns away and you are not obedient, and if you are drawn away to bow down to other Gods and worship them, I declare to you this day that you will certainly be destroyed ... This day I call the heavens and the earth as witnesses against you that I have set before you life and death, blessings and curses. Now choose life so that you and your children may live, and that you may love the LORD your God, listen to His voice, and hold fast to HIM. For the LORD is your life and He will give you many years in the land..."
> (Deuteronomy 30:14-20)

The challenge is set before us all. Everyone, not just community leaders, not just family leaders, not just enterprise leaders, but all are challenged to live in relationship with the LORD. This includes all of life, not just in religious practice, but in community, in work, in leisure, in family, in public and in private, we are challenged to listen to His Word, to discern what to do and thus to obey His guidance. He is Lord of all!

REFLECTIONS

The Ten Commandments:

Re-read the Ten Commandments in Exodus 20. Ask the question:

What is the undergirding principle or value behind each commandment?

The government of our country:

Think of the legislative, the administrative and judiciary branches of government.

In what ways does the nation in which we live line up with (or not fit) the overall structures instituted in the law of Moses?

The government of our social or corporate organisation:

We all find ourselves involved in and impacted by various social structures. These may include family, employment/work, financial, leisure/sport, community service, church, nation or whatever. Each setting has its unique way of being structured. In each setting there are spoken or unspoken 'ground rules'. There are ways in which the functions of the group are conducted. There are ways to deal with the more challenging situations.

In what way are the principles behind the way God structured the nation of Israel applicable to our social group?

How is the vision, the overall purpose of the organisation, commonly discussed?

Have I consciously thought through the ground rules of my social group?

How have those rules of behaviour been articulated or communicated in a way that inspires unity and that works positively to achieve the group's purposes?

How could this be more intentionally done?

What can I do better?

The government of our Christian organisation:

Is the group overtly Christian?

If so, how is an awareness of God and His purposes evident in its structure, goals and practices?

How do we follow through with functions that fit in with the spirit and principles behind the law of Moses?

4

THE RISE AND FALL OF A NATION

This chapter describes Israel's attempts to enact the rule of God's law.

What makes a nation great?

When Donald Trump campaigned for the presidency of the United States of America, he used the slogan "Make America great again". It is not for me to judge whether his presidency has helped make America a greater nation, but it does raise the question: "What does make a nation great?"

The Bible emphatically says that *righteousness* exalts a nation, but sin condemns any people (Proverbs 14:34). This proverb clearly states that the spiritual or moral condition of the people determines the success or prosperity of a nation. The degree of the people's righteousness directly affects the degree of a nation's flourishing.

What is righteousness? It can be said that righteousness has three aspects:

- right *standing*, living in right relationship to God,
- right *doing*, living uprightly, and
- right *dealing*, acting justly.

People who live in right relationship with God are at peace with Him. They understand that He is king. He is to be listened to, talked to and obeyed. They hearken to the voice of God. They are His children, and they outwork that relationship, walking 'hand in hand' with Him.

People who do right are those who know what God has said is right and what is wrong, and are committed to following His way, living in purity of attitude and action. This is often referred to as 'morality'. I hesitate to use this word, as it implies that the criteria for what is deemed good comes from social mores or community consensus rather than what God says is true and right.

People who deal right are those who act justly. They have embraced God's heart for justice and make choices that are for the good of others. An outworking of the righteousness of God is sacrificially loving others, positively outworking God's justice and grace. As will be noted later, this area of social justice has been taken up by many as a major focus or role of government.

The challenge to be righteous is the responsibility of everyone. We are all created in the image of God. That means we are equally responsible and free to do what is right. To be created in the image of God means that we are all accountable to Him. It also means that corporately we are created to be responsible, to respond together to do what is right. Leaders need to be just. They may have the power to protect our freedom to do what is right, but it is not the obligation of only those in leadership positions to be righteous. When it comes to righteousness, we are all responsible, accountable to God. We all affect the wellbeing of others, the common good. We all contribute to the flourishing of the community and the nation.

The curse of national unrighteousness

Genesis 18 records a conversation between God and Abraham about the fate of the city of Sodom. God reflects on the future nation of Abraham's descendants. He says:

> I have chosen (Abraham), so that he will direct his children and his household after him to keep the way of the LORD by doing what is right and just, so that the LORD will bring about for Abraham what He has promised him. (Genesis 18:19)

The outworking of the blessing was dependent on the righteousness of the people of the nation. In contrast, the unrighteousness of Sodom and Gomorrah necessitated God bringing upon them His just judgement. Abraham discussed with God what it would take to save the city from destruction. What was the minimum number of righteous people in the city that would save it from destruction? It seems that a 'critical mass' of righteousness would save the city, and blessing or cursing of a nation depends on the righteousness of the people.

Sin and righteousness in the time of Joshua and the judges

The history of ancient Israel as recorded in the Bible illustrates well this correlation between righteousness and flourishing. It is the main theme of the books of history (Joshua through to Esther) in the Old Testament.

The book of Joshua tells the story of the nation re-entering, conquering and re-occupying the promised land. God instructed the people to completely remove the temporary occupiers of the land. Critics of biblical faith try to make this out to be hideous ethnic cleansing! But it was not. It was about removing unrighteousness.

As previously described in Genesis, the Canaanites were typical of the peoples of the time.

> The LORD saw how great the wickedness of the human race had become on the earth, and that every inclination of the thoughts of the human heart was only evil all the time. (Genesis 6:5)

> Now the earth was corrupt in God's sight and was full of violence... (Genesis 6:11)

They were subject to the wrath of God, the consequences of their Godless lifestyle – misery, disease and death. God's intent was that the nation of Israel would live out the life prescribed in the law without the polluting influence of evil anti-God ideas and behaviour. The purpose was to eliminate intrenched ideas that work against the knowledge of God (cf 2 Corinthians 10:5). Canaanites such as Rahab, who chose to be on God's side, were not expelled but welcomed into the community (Joshua 5 & 6). Expelling people was to facilitate the elimination of unrighteousness, evil thoughts and practices from the nation.

In this process of eliminating unrighteousness, the first challenge facing Joshua and the people was the city of Jericho. Before giving His instructions, the commander of the heavenly army, the Lord Himself met with Joshua and made it clear that He was not on the side of either group of people per se, but rather Israel was to choose to live on His side by humbly submitting to Him and His instructions. The nation would be great in battle when they chose His righteousness and followed His instructions. When they did this, they were successful and when they did not, they failed. God conquered Jericho when the nation committed themselves to follow His instructions (Joshua 5 & 6). Then, when someone did not obey, they failed at the next challenge at Ai (Joshua 7). When they failed to inquire of the Lord, they were deceived by the Gibeonites (Joshua 9). The flourishing of their success went hand in hand with the righteousness of living in right relationship with the LORD.

In Joshua chapter 24, when Joshua was dying, he challenged the people on the core issue determining the future of the nation. It was not the defence of the borders. It was not the integrity of the economy. It was not the freedom of the citizens, nor their commitment to social justice. These were all vital, but not the core issue. The core commitment was whom they would serve. Joshua was adamant they understood their commitment to listen to and obey the LORD. Get this right and all the other outcomes would follow. Each generation of Israelites would need to follow through this commitment, and then they would flourish. Get it wrong and God would not bless them.

The book of Judges relates what happened in the years after Moses and Joshua. The first generation who lived during the time of Joshua followed the way of the Lord, but they failed to teach the next generation. The story of the time of 'the judges' is summarised like this:

> ...another generation grew up who knew neither the Lord nor what he had done for Israel. Then the Israelites did evil in the eyes of the Lord and ... followed and worshiped various gods of the people around them ... the LORD gave them into the hands of raiders ... and sold them into the hands of their enemies... They were in great distress...
>
> Then the LORD raised up judges who saved them out of the hands of these raiders... But when the judge died ... they refused to give up their stubborn ways... (See Judges 2:10-19)

The story relates a series of cycles in the life of the nation: sinning, suffering, supplication, and salvation through the work of a judge God gave them.

Passage	Suffering under	Period	Judge (rescuer/leader)
3:5-11	Mesopotamia	8 yrs	Othniel
3:12-31	Moab	18 yrs	Ehud, Shamgar
4:1-5:31	Canaan	20 yrs	Deborah, Barak
6:1-8:35	Midianites	7 yrs	Gideon
9:1-10:5	Anarchy, Abimelech		Tolah, Jair
10:6-12:7	Philistines and others	18 yrs	Jephthah, Ibzan, Elon, Abdon
13:1-16:31	Philistines	40 yrs	Samson

The book of Judges notes that "in those days Israel had no king". When they rejected the rule of God, they did 'what was right in their own eyes' (See Judges 17:6 and 21:25). That sounds very much like the spirit of the initial fall – choosing for themselves what was good or evil, following their own inclinations about right and wrong.

Representing God, each of these judges acted as a temporary de facto king. Sometimes their leadership was effective. They led the people back into some relationship to God. Sometimes their leadership was found wanting.

The flourishing of the people was like a rollercoaster. They were up when they and their leader followed God's way and God's leading, and they were down when they did not.

Sin, righteousness and kings

As recorded in the last chapters of Genesis, Israel, in his last days, prophesied that from the descendants of Judah there would be kings in Israel, in anticipation of the coming of the rightful deliverer and king of all (Genesis 49:9-12). God gave instructions in the law about what they and the king should do when this scenario eventuated (Deuteronomy 17:14-20). The king was not to accumulate large amounts of personal wealth, prestige and power. He was to daily read a personal copy of the law of God and so learn to always revere God. The LORD, not the human king, was to be exalted above all the people.

It was not until many years later that the people of Israel chose to have a king rather than take responsibility to rule themselves. The last of the judges was the prophet Samuel. In 1 Samuel chapter 8 we read that the people came to Samuel requesting him to "appoint a king to lead us, such as all the other nations have" (1 Samuel 8:5). Samuel was displeased with the people's request, and so he prayed. God told him that they were not rejecting him, that is Samuel and his sons. Rather they were rejecting Him, that is the LORD, as their king. Up to this time, whenever they recognised God as their king and heeded His voice, they flourished. It seems that the people of Israel did not want to be responsible to listen to the voice of God through the law but rather wanted to be told what to do by a human king. They wanted central control of government rather than local administration of the law. They failed to appoint local judges as instructed in Deuteronomy 16, but rather looked to Samuel as their national judge. They did not want to trust in God to enable them to defend themselves against foreign enemies. They wanted a national military force. Rather than trusting God, they wanted a king to fight their battles.

In short, they rejected the government of self-responsibility, being personally accountable to God, and wanted the 'government' of another human to be responsible for their wellbeing.

God allowed this compromise. In fact, He ordained it to be so. If the people were not up to the responsibility of self-government, they needed a king to govern them. But it would come at a price. There would be a burgeoning public service and oppressive taxes to fund the kings servants (1 Samuel 8:10-18). This would especially be so if the king was like the kings of other nations, centred on personal power and prestige rather than the good of all the people and the glory of God. And that was the nature of their first king, Saul.

The biblical narrative continues to describe kings who did good and kings who did evil. The kings who did what was 'right in the eyes of the LORD', did what pleased God and what was best for the common good or flourishing of the people. However, even these good kings were unable to always resist doing what pleased themselves. The great warrior-king, David, is an eminent example of this. The book of 2 Samuel describes the time of his reign. Firstly, David and his men had to fight against the house of Saul for many months to establish David's rule over the whole of Israel, not just the tribe of Judah. Then he expanded their kingdom's territory into land occupied by other people groups, particularly to the north. When David followed the word of the Lord, he and the nation flourished. When he sinned, as described in the latter part of 2 Samuel, there were troubles.

The City of God

To have a king and a kingdom "such as the other nations have", Israel needed a city to be the 'seat of power'. One of the first things David did as king was to defeat the Jebusites who lived in Jerusalem. He captured the fortress of Zion which became called the City of David (2 Samuel 5:6-10).

Jerusalem was built and occupied by Canaanites. It was a city which originated like any other city. In the time of Abraham it was called Salem and was ruled by Melchizedek, the priest of El, the most high God, the Canaanite god who most resembled God Almighty. But it was still a city of the world until God led David to adopt it as the City of God. Its focus was to be the LORD, with the centrality of the temple, which was to be built there. The king and the people were to exemplify learning and obeying God's law.

Jerusalem was to be a signal or witness to all other cities of how God would deal with them, for better or worse, according to their righteousness. It could be a lighthouse city, exemplifying the blessing of God on the people. On the other hand, if it failed to follow the LORD, it could exemplify the curse of sinning with internal strife, violence, disease and destruction. Even though Jerusalem was the adopted City of God, it was still subject to the same accountability as any other city. God would not unconditionally bless the city. It was the responsibility of the city to bless the LORD.

National accountability

The ongoing story of ancient Israel under the leadership of kings reflects much the same pattern as when they had judges. The writers of the books of Kings and Chronicles highlight how some kings did what was right in God's eyes and others did not. There was prosperity when the king and the people followed the LORD. There was decline and suffering and ultimate subjection to enemies when they did not.

The nature of leadership of the kings varied from king to king. Some were humble before God and the nation flourished. Some began well, like Solomon who prayed:

> "Give me an understanding heart so that I can govern your people well and know the difference between right and wrong. For who by himself is able to govern this great people of yours?" (1 Kings 3:9)

But then he did not finish well. Other kings were self-seeking and oppressive, and the nation suffered. Some kings, such as Josiah (See 2 Kings 21), revived the reading and learning of the law of God. This enabled the people to choose to do what was right according to God. When they did, there was greater freedom and prosperity.

At times when they did not follow the Lord's way, and were sinful, following their own lusts, God raised up a prophet to speak His message to them. The stories of Elijah and Elisha, as recorded in the books of Kings, illustrate this well.

Isaiah prophesied profusely against the unrighteousness of

the nation. He described its unrighteousness and spoke of the consequent judgement of God. For example, in Isaiah chapter 5, he said:

...he [the LORD Almighty] looked for justice,
but saw bloodshed;
for righteousness, but heard cries of distress. (7b)

So people will be brought low and everyone humbled... (15a)

Woe to those who call evil good and good evil,
Who put darkness for light and light for darkness,
Who put bitter for sweet and sweet for bitter.

Woe to those who are wise in their own eyes
and clever in their own sight. (20-21)

Another example is Micah, who was sent by God to address the sin of the kingdoms of Israel and Judah. The northern kingdom of Israel especially had abandoned God and His law. The rich and powerful were exploiting the poor and living a life of self-indulgence. Micah warned them of pending destruction, corresponding to their unrighteousness. God judges a society on the way they treat the poor and the marginalised. Micah challenged them to repent.

The judgement of God on the city of Jerusalem and the nations of Judah and Israel is a common theme of the latter prophets (see Micah 3:9-12, Ezekiel 16, and Jeremiah 13:8-11).

At times of stubborn sinning, God raised up an authoritarian king who ruled in a heavy-handed way, or raised up a foreign enemy who conquered and oppressed them. The king Jehu is an example of such an aggressive, ungodly ruler doing God's business (see 2 Kings 9 and 10). God raised up unrighteous regimes from within the nation, and others from without, like the Assyrians and the Babylonians, to fulfil His purposes. Whichever way, God gave them (as with the other nations of the world) the political leadership they needed to achieve His purposes.

Sin, righteousness and a fitting government

Reflecting on the message of the story of the ancient nation of Israel and their various kings, one could ask the question: What is the best form of government for a nation?

Throughout history the most common nature of government has been authoritarian. The king, emperor or ruling group has had absolute authority. Effectively it was the rule of the strong gang leader who could organise his gang members to suppress challenges to his leadership. The military, whether it be knights, the army or navy, were the leader's enforcers.

In the ancient Middle East, some kings developed a law code vaguely similar, but not as comprehensive, to that which was instituted in Israel. For example, the Babylonian king, Hammurabi, is known for his law code inscribed on a plinth. Hammurabi used this set of rules to aid his control of the people. We read in the biblical books of Daniel and Esther about the law of the Medes and Persians. It seems that in this regime the king had advisors who shaped up laws upon which the king could put his authoritative seal of approval.

In Rome, instead of one person ruling, a group of elite older men called the Senate ruled the city. This was called a republic – the leadership came from the people (the public). In some Greek cities, an assembly of eligible adult men discussed and instituted the laws for the city. In recent times this arrangement has been described as the world's first form of 'democracy'. The word democracy originally means rulership of or by the people. In reality, in these Greek cities, it was only about 20 percent of the local adult population who were eligible to have any say in these assemblies.

At the beginning of the 21st century, the nation of Iraq was ruled by a strongman. Many citizens suffered at his hand. Some Western leaders perceived that he was dangerous and that he needed to be removed from power. The ensuing war quickly ousted the dictator, and a form of 'democracy' was installed. Despite the continued presence of the Western military to help maintain stability, evil expressed itself in the nation with the rise of groups such as ISIS. It could be asked, "Were the people of the nation better off?" It could be argued that despite the evil oppression of the strongman, he was there serving a purpose that 'democracy' could not deliver.

God will determine that a nation gets the government it needs.

God gives a nation a government which best fits their virtue and wisdom. When Israel did not rise to the responsibility of governing themselves under the rule of God, they needed a king to rule over them. When they were comparatively self-disciplined, the king could rule with a light hand. They flourished and enjoyed freedom in line with the degree of their righteousness. When they grievously sinned, they were controlled by a despotic king or a foreign oppressor. As we said at the beginning of this chapter, righteousness exalts a nation (Proverbs 14:34). Unrighteousness incurs oppression.

This applied not only to Israel. The story of Jonah relates how the people of Nineveh, enemies of Israel were saved from peril when they repented of their wrong ways.

Surely a nation is great when the people are righteous. This will only be fully realised when God ultimately fulfills His kingdom of righteousness, about which the latter prophets and the New Testament have much to say.

REFLECTIONS

Self-reflection:

Re-visit the description of righteousness at the beginning of this chapter.

In what way does your way of life embody these three aspects of righteousness?

A righteous life begins with a relationship with God (See John 1:12,13).

How is your ongoing relationship with Him going?

Is it affecting your attitude toward and relationship with others?

When you are aware there is a problem in the community:

Do you find yourself blaming someone else for the problems you or your community experience?

How often is that someone else to blame a leader – your parent, your pastor, your club president, your city mayor, your national leader, the government?

How can you first check if it's you that can make a change?

What can you do to contribute to the answer?

Being proactive toward community wellbeing:

In what ways do you take responsibility for your personal wellbeing?

How do you take responsibility for contributing to your community's wellbeing?

Reflecting on the state of the nation:

Have you noticed the ever-increasing multitude of rules and regulations in our current nation?

Is there a connection between the need for these regulations and the righteousness of the people?

How could this trend be reversed?

How might *we* contribute to this reversal?

5

THE PROMISED KING

The king of the psalmists and prophets

Many of the Psalms are written by David who was the king of Israel, and yet he and the other psalmists recognised and worshipped God as their king. Here are a few examples:

> Hear my cry for help, my King, and my God, for to you I pray… (Psalm 5:2)

> The Lord is King for ever and ever… (Psalm 10:16)

> For dominion belongs to the LORD and He rules over the nations. (Psalm 22:28)

> Lift up your heads, you gates…
> that the king of glory may come in.
> Who is this King of glory?
> The LORD strong and mighty,
> the LORD mighty in battle…

The LORD Almighty –
he is the King of glory. (Psalm 24:7-10)

For God is the king of all the earth;
sing to Him a psalm of praise.
God reigns over the nations;
God is seated on His holy throne. (Psalm 47:7-8)

The LORD has established His throne in heaven,
and His kingdom rules over all. (Psalm 103:19)

I will exalt you, my God the King;
I will praise your name for ever and ever. (Psalm 145:1)

In the same way, the prophets spoke of God:

I am the LORD, your Holy One,
Israel's Creator your King. (Isaiah 43:15)

No one is like you, LORD… King of the nations…
But the LORD is the true God;
he is the living God, the eternal King…
(Jeremiah 10:7-10)

Jeremiah repeatedly refers to God as "the King, whose name is the LORD Almighty".

The story of Daniel chapter 4 graphically affirms the rightful place of God in relationship to the kings of this world.

The king of Babylon said:

> To the peoples, nations and men of every language,
> who live in all the world:
> May you prosper greatly!
> It is my pleasure to tell you about the miraculous signs
> and wonders that the most high god has performed
> for me.
> How great are his signs,
> how mighty his wonders!
> His kingdom is an everlasting kingdom;
> his dominion endures from generation to generation.
> (Daniel 4:1-3)

What led to this declaration by Nebuchadnezzar, who was king of Babylon, the dominant empire at that time? He had a dream which the prophet Daniel interpreted for him. What Daniel told him came to pass a year later. As he was on the roof of the royal palace he said to himself, "Is not this the great Babylon I have built as the royal residence, by mighty power and for the glory of my majesty?" (Daniel 4:30)

A voice came from heaven, and told him his authority would be taken away until:

> ...you acknowledge that the Most High is sovereign over the kingdoms of men and gives them to anyone he wishes. (Daniel 4:32)

Nebuchadnezzar immediately was driven away and lived like a wild animal. At the end of that time his sanity was restored, and he declared:

Then I praised the Most High;
I honoured and glorified him who lives forever.
His dominion is an eternal dominion,
His kingdom endures from generation to generation...
(Daniel 4:34-35)

Now I, Nebuchadnezzar, praise and exalt and glorify the King of Heaven,
because everything he does is right and all his ways are just.
And those who walk in pride he is able to humble.
(Daniel 4:37)

What a great proclamation of the sovereignty of God, the King of all kings! It is to be noted that when Nebuchadnezzar recognised God as the higher authority over all kings he then wished for the prosperity of all the people rather than just himself. As in the promise of blessing given to Abraham, there is a positive 'domino effect' of blessing when God is recognised in His rightful place.

The prophetic promise of a king

The role of a prophet is to speak out the specific word of God to the people of their time.
The message of the latter prophets in Israel included:

- alerting the people to their unrighteousness,

- warning them of the consequences of their unrighteousness,
- challenging them to repent and turn their lives around, and
- promising the blessings that follow repentance.

In addition to this message that had immediate application and challenge for the hearers of their time, many of the latter prophets promised a future time of restoration of the nation. A remnant of God's people would return to faithfully keep His covenant, living righteously, and would be returned to prosperity. Included in these promises are the description of a great deliverer, leader and king. Israel would be ruled by a righteous king and through this king would come a blessing to all the people of the earth. The following is a sample of these prophecies:

> For unto us a child is born, to us a son is given,
> And the government will be on his shoulders.
> And he will be called Wonderful Counsellor,
> Mighty God, Everlasting Father, Prince of Peace.
> Of the greatness of his government and peace there will be no end
> He will reign on David's throne and over his kingdom,
> Establishing and uphold it with justice and righteousness from that time on and forever.
> The zeal of the Lord Almighty will accomplish this.
> (Isaiah 9:6-7)

Isaiah spoke of a coming kingdom of righteousness, with a king and just co-rulers:

> See, a king will reign in righteousness and rulers will rule with justice. (Isaiah 32:1)

> Your eyes will see the king in his beauty... (Isaiah 33:17)

Jeremiah also spoke on these lines:

> "The days are coming," declares the Lord, "when I will raise up for [or from] David a righteous branch, a king who will reign wisely and do what is just and right in the land..." (Jeremiah 23:5).

In Jeremiah chapter 37, the prophet speaks of a time when God's people would be gathered from their dispersion around the world and they would be one nation ruled by one king. They would live righteously and "David my servant will be king over them", and they would live in peace and prosperity.

Hosea speaks of a future restoration along these lines:

> The people of Judah and the people of Israel will come together, they will appoint one leader... (Hosea 1:11)

> Afterwards the Israelites will return and seek the Lord their God and David their king... (Hosea 3:5)

Ezekiel's prophecies about Israel include:

> There will be one king over all of them ... they will no longer defile themselves ... with any of their offences, for I will save them from all their sinful backsliding, and I will cleanse them. They will be my people and I will be their God. My servant David will be king over them, and they will all have one shepherd... They and their children and their children's children will live there forever, and David my servant will, be their prince forever...
> (Ezekiel 37:21-28)

Daniel was told that the nation of the Jews would be restored for a time of 'seventy weeks' for the purpose of receiving the coming Messiah, the anointed deliverer (Daniel 9:25,26).

Who was this coming anointed one, this Messiah?

Several of the above passages refer to the Messiah as 'David' or 'of David'. They point to the king being a descendant of David.

They speak of him in terms of beauty, glory and righteousness. The latter parts of the prophesies of Isaiah are an eminent example of the promise of the righteous king who will restore righteousness in all aspects of the nation to the glory of God.

The prophets identify him as the LORD Himself, as some of the above quotes say, and as these examples say:

> For the LORD is our judge,
> The LORD is our lawgiver,

The LORD is our King,
It is He who will save us. (Isaiah 33:22)

Israel's King and Redeemer, the LORD Almighty...
(Isaiah 44:6)

...then you will know that I, the Lord, am your Saviour,
your Redeemer, the Mighty One of Jacob...
No longer will violence be heard in your land,
no ruin or destruction within your borders,
...the LORD will be your everlasting light, and your days
of sorrow will end.
Then all your people will be righteous and they will
possess the land forever... (Isaiah 60:16-22)

The LORD will be King over the whole earth.
On that day there will be one LORD,
and His name the only name. (Zechariah 14:9)

How would the Messiah achieve dominion?

These prophesies of the Messiah speak of his power and glory, but there is no reference to him using human military power. Then there are other rather different descriptions of the work of the Messiah. The titles given to the Messiah in Isaiah 9 are:

Wonderful Counsellor: A counsellor is an advisor not a controller. A counsellor leads someone to choose for themselves to follow his or her advice.

Mighty God: A Mighty God is a strongman, who has the power to enforce, but engenders worship. People willingly follow.

Everlasting Father: A father is an honoured benevolent protector and nurturer. He is honoured by the wisdom and integrity of his son.

Prince of Peace: A prince of peace is an overseer of health and prosperity. The Hebrew word for peace is shalom and means reconciliation and flourishing. It is achieved, not by separation from potential conflict, but by reconciliation. The prince of peace is therefore not an enforcer but a reconciler and peacemaker.

The Messiah King is also referred to as a *suffering servant* and *caring shepherd*:

> See, my servant will act wisely,
> he will be raised and lifted up, and highly exalted...
> he grew up before him like a tender shoot,
> and like a root out of dry ground.
> He had no beauty or majesty to attract us to him.
> He was despised and rejected by mankind,
> a man of suffering and familiar with pain.
> Like one from whom people hide their faces,
> he was despised and we held him in low esteem...
> (Isaiah 52 and 53)
>
> Rejoice greatly, daughter Zion!

> Shout, Daughter Jerusalem!
> See, your king comes to you,
> Righteous and victorious,
> Lowly and riding on a donkey,
> On a colt, the foal of a donkey.
> I will take away the chariots from Ephraim
> and the warhorses from Jerusalem,
> and the battle bow will be broken.
> He will proclaim peace to the nations.
> His rule will extend from sea to sea
> And from the river to the ends of the earth.
> (Zechariah 9:9,10)

and,

> The LORD their God will save His people on that day
> As a shepherd saves his flock... (Zechariah 9:16)

Here is a picture of power and glory and humble service and suffering in the same person!

We are left wondering what the hearers of the prophets made of all this! What is the nature of this kingdom? How will it be inaugurated? How will the king exercise his power? What will it look like in everyday life?

Meanwhile God was saying, "Watch this space!"

REFLECTIONS

About Jews anticipating the Messiah:

Imagine you are a Jew living in Israel several centuries on from the prophets, but before the arrival of Jesus.

What sort of deliverer would you be anticipating?

Would you find the various prophecies confusing? List his characteristics.

How do you think he would achieve dominion over Israel and humanity?

How do you think his kingdom would operate?

About a national anthem:

New Zealanders are blessed with a national anthem which begins with the words, "God of nations, at thy feet…" It is a prayer of unified submission to God. It is worth examining the words of all the verses. (See the appendix for the words of all the verses.)

What do these words tell us about the thinking of the people who chose this song to be the anthem of New Zealand?

Reflecting back on the principles described in the first five chapters of this book, make a comparison of the New Zealand anthem with biblical principles about God's purposes for nations. Try making a list of these.

Is there something not in these lyrics that you would like to be there?

Are there some words that you think are inconsistent with biblical principles?

About praying for the nations:

As Christians, let's pray for our nation and other nations of the world. Why not pray now?

6

THE GOOD NEWS OF THE KINGDOM OF GOD

As a result of the prophesies about the coming king, there developed in Israel an expectation of the coming of an anointed one, a messiah, a deliverer king. They expected this king would be a mighty warrior or political deliverer. He would come and usher in 'the kingdom of heaven'. This expression 'the kingdom of heaven' (*malkut samayim* in Hebrew) as such is not found in the Old Testament scriptures but is very much entrenched in the thinking and language of the Jews by the time of Jesus' coming.

The kingdom of heaven is very much the main theme of the teaching of Jesus as related in the synoptic gospels, Matthew, Mark and Luke. Matthew, writing to mainly Jews, uses the expression 'kingdom of heaven', most likely because Jews avoided the direct use of the name of God. It is assumed that Jesus would have used the Aramaic words for kingdom of heaven. Mark and Luke were writing mainly to Gentiles and so used the expression kingdom of God, as this would be more meaningful to them.

The very beginning of Matthew, introducing the genealogy of Jesus, reads:

> A record of the genealogy of Jesus Christ [Messiah], the son of David, the son of Abraham. (Matthew 1:1)

When one reads the whole of Matthew, it is clear that his main theme is presenting Jesus as the son of David, the Messiah, the King of the Jews. For this reason, much of the discussion in this chapter follows the Gospel of Matthew.

Matthew frequently adds to a description of an event in the life of Jesus a comment that this fulfilled what was said (by God) through a prophet. When telling the story of the conception of Jesus he makes the first of these references to the prophets, referring to Isaiah chapter 7. It is Matthew who tells the story of the wise men who were seeking the king who was to come, and the threat this idea posed to King Herod. The references to messianic prophecies continue through Matthew's gospel.

Entering the kingdom

At the beginning of Matthew comes the story of John the Baptist:

> John the Baptist came, preaching ... and saying, "Repent for the kingdom of heaven is near." This is he who was spoken of through the prophet Isaiah... (Matthew 3:1,2)

In response to the soon coming kingdom, John did not make a call to prepare arms for battle to win the Messiah's war. Rather, he urged a change of heart, repentance that is demonstrated by baptism.

Jesus began his preaching with the same call:

"Repent, for the kingdom of heaven is near." (Matthew 4:17)

Talking to Nicodemus, a Jewish teacher, Jesus immediately speaks of entering the kingdom of God:

"Very truly, I tell you, no one can see the kingdom of God unless they are born again (or from above)... Very truly I tell you, none can enter the kingdom of God unless they are born of water and the Spirit..." (John 3:3-8)

Spiritual birth is the entry point into the kingdom of God.

Living in the kingdom

In chapters 5 to 7, Matthew summarises Jesus' teaching of how to live in the kingdom by relating what is known as the Sermon on the Mount. His position on a mount echoes the giving of the law of Moses from the mountain. The sermon does not begin with a call to political action. Rather it is an affirmation of right attitudes of the heart, such as humility, sorrow, meekness, diligence, kindness and sincerity. The kingdom of heaven works inside out – attitudes first, then action. The first and last of these 'beatitudes' have the suffix 'for theirs is the kingdom of heaven". Even these two attitudes are not of arrogance and aggressive dominion. Rather they are:

> "Blessed are the poor in spirit," [and] "Blessed are those who are persecuted because of righteousness." (Matthew 5:3,10)

The sermon continues this theme, highlighting attitudes backed up with corresponding action. Right from the beginning of his teaching, He makes the point that the 'method' of the kingdom is not a new set of rules or laws, replacing the old, but rather the outworking of an attitude of humility, faith and sacrificial love. The 'Lord's Prayer' reflects these kingdom attitudes. The king is to be honoured. The kingdom is the will of the Father being done, on earth as it is in heaven. It involves trusting God for daily needs and trusting Him for deliverance when the going gets tough. It involves forgiveness. It involves prayer, living in relationship with the Father, and its object is the glory of God... (See Matthew 6:9-13.)

Living in the kingdom is not just following the letter of the law of God, but having the right attitude that underpins the doing of the law. Living in the kingdom is not living in fear of the future, but rather trusting God. It is the righteousness of sacrificially giving to those in need, without seeking recognition. It is seeking His kingdom and His righteousness, and God will see that other necessities of this life will fall into place. Living in the kingdom is not critically judging others. It is God's prerogative to judge. While being discerning of those who speak falsehoods, we are called to be single-minded, pursuing the core truth, not peripheral issues. It is building on a solid foundation, not the sand on the side.

Living in the kingdom is not a matter of: "Show me the rules and I will obey", but rather: "Show me the king and I will follow in relationship with Him". In John 10, Jesus used the analogy of the ancient shepherd leading his sheep who follow him because they know his voice.

> "I am the good shepherd; I know my sheep, and my sheep know me." (John 15:14)

Identifying the King

Matthew continues his account with stories of miracles which fulfil the words of the prophets and discussions and teaching which demonstrate Jesus practised what he preached about the kingdom.

The miracles were signs of his identity. Followers of John the Baptist came to him asking,

> Are you the one who was to come, or should we expect someone else? Jesus replied, "Go back to John and report what you hear and see: the blind receive sight, the lame walk, those who have leprosy are cured, the deaf hear, the dead are raised, and the good news is preached to the poor"... (Matthew 11:3-6)

On one occasion Jesus provoked a discussion with his disciples about his identity. They offered the opinions of others and so Jesus asked: "Who do you say that I am?" Peter answered: "You are the Messiah, the Son of the living God." Jesus points out to him that this understanding of his identity comes from God not from hearsay. This is the foundation upon which He will assemble His church, the people in the kingdom. To them He will give 'the keys of the kingdom', that is the authority over spiritual powers. He asked his disciples to allow God to reveal His identity to others (Matthew 16:13-20).

Jesus, the king, wants people to recognise him as King, not through verbal or political persuasion, but by spiritual revelation. Compliance to the king is a matter of the heart not overt coercion.

The nature and method of the kingdom

The Messiah King revealed his identity and practised his dominion, not by exercising military or political power, but by loving people, meeting their needs. Serving for the good of the people it seems is the method of his dominion.

While speaking about the greatness of John the Baptist, Jesus said that the least in the kingdom of heaven is greater than John the Baptist. Jesus implied that the kingdom of heaven now being inaugurated was something superior to all previous kingdoms in this world. And then he said:

> From the days of John the Baptist until now, the kingdom of heaven has been subjected to violence, and violent people have been raiding it. (Matthew 11:12)

People had been trying to bring it into being by overt forceful means. Jesus was saying that this is not the nature of the kingdom of heaven. It is not achieved by military or strong political means. Jesus was declaring a new way.

At His trial, Pilate asked Jesus, "Are you the king of the Jews?" Jesus led Pilate to admit that this question was instigated by His Jewish accusers. Then Jesus said:

> My kingdom is not of this world. If it were, my servants would fight to prevent my arrest by the Jewish leaders. But now my kingdom is from another place. (John 18:36)

The parables of the kingdom

Matthew's account of many of Jesus' parables are often prefaced with "The kingdom of heaven is like...", and the accompanying discussion is usually about the nature of the kingdom, both in the present and "at the end of the age." In the present, the kingdom is not observed universally. There are productive and unproductive soils. There are weeds and good wheat. The kingdom is growing like a mustard tree. It is scattered in the world like yeast. Like seeking a treasure or a precious pearl, the kingdom of heaven is desiring the king and gaining him, whatever the sacrificial cost. In some parables, the kingdom is like serving the master, the king. At the end of the age, it will be like a harvest of wheat or of fish in a net, like a separating of the weeds from the good grain, like a separation of the sheep from the goats, like workers receiving their pay at the end of the day, and like a wedding feast when the bride is united with the groom. It is like welcoming home a lost son, and like paying extravagant wages to late-coming workers, the reward of living in the kingdom is the undeserved grace of the king.

The citizens of the kingdom

The common perception of the Jews in Jesus' time was that the kingdom of heaven would be populated by and run by successful law-keeping Jews. Jesus let them know they had it wrong.

When the disciples tried to prevent people bringing little children to him, he said:

> Let the little children come to me, and do not hinder them, for the kingdom of heaven belongs to such as these. (Matthew 19:14)

He was making it clear that simple submissive faith characterises members of the kingdom.

Then a rich man came wanting to know what he could do to earn eternal life. Jesus reminded him of his desire to keep all the law of Moses and then struck at his prior commitment – his material wealth. Selling all his possessions and giving the money to the poor was too much! When he went away, Jesus said:

> Truly I tell you, it is hard for someone who is rich to

enter the kingdom of heaven. Again I tell you, it is easier for a camel to go through the eye of a needle than for someone who is rich to enter the kingdom of God. (Matthew 19:23,24)

The kingdom is reserved for those who are prepared to abandon everything and allow the Spirit to make the LORD king of their lives. It takes a miracle to achieve the otherwise impossible.

To point out that the citizenship of the kingdom was not just Jews, Jesus told the parable of the treacherous tenants who killed the son of the landlord. Those who rejected Him as their master and turned against Him would be replaced by others.

Therefore, I tell you that the kingdom of God will be taken away from you and given to a people who will produce its fruit... (Matthew 21:43)

Jesus made it very clear that His kingdom was to be non-national, transcending ethnicities and cultures. His kingdom would be a 'subversive' or infiltrating power in all nations. His kingdom would be multicultural. His rulership internally in the hearts of the citizens would be expressed in various cultural forms. His kingdom would be executed by the power of the Spirit from within, not by human coercion or threatening persuasion.

The greatest in the kingdom

When the disciples asked Jesus who was the greatest in the kingdom, he replied:

> Truly I tell you, unless you change and become like little children, you will never enter the kingdom of heaven. Therefore, whoever takes the lowly position of this child is the greatest in the kingdom of heaven. And whoever welcomes one such child in my name welcomes me. (Matthew 18:1-5)

The mother of James and John wanted Jesus to assign them positions in the kingdom of heaven right next to the King Jesus. Jesus said, effectively, that they misunderstood the nature of the kingdom, and that achievement in the kingdom entailed humble sacrifice. This interaction provoked an adverse reaction by the other disciples. Jesus called them aside and said:

> You know that the rulers of the Gentiles lord it over them, and their high officials exercise authority over them. Not so with you. Instead, whoever wants to be first among you must be your servant, and whoever wants to be first must be your slave – just as the Son of Man did not come to be served, but to serve, and give his life as a ransom for many. (See Matthew 20:20-28)

This certainly exemplifies the difference between the kingdoms of this world and the kingdom of heaven. Vying for leadership and exercising lordship over others is the way of the world. The greatest in the kingdom are those who humbly accept His grace and sacrificially serve. It is an upside-down kingdom. Not only is the kingdom of heaven inside out, but it is upside down.

> So the last will be first and the first will be last. (Matthew 20:16)

Preparing for the full realisation of the kingdom

Immediately before Jesus' arrest and crucifixion, Jesus told parables of the kingdom that are about the time when the king will come to reign at the restoration of all things (see Matthew 21, 22 and 25). The main point of each of these parables is not the details of what will happen at that time, but rather about the preparedness of those anticipating Christ's return, about what is done in the here and now. The challenge is extended to all of us. Are we like the foolish virgins who were unprepared or like the wise ones who were prepared with extra oil for their lamps? Are we prepared to endure over a long time if needed? Preparedness for the kingdom involves vigilance and endurance. Are we like the servant who did not know the character of his master, or are we like the five and two talented servants who knew their master personally, knew his gracious character, and faithfully used their gifts for the expansion of his kingdom? Are we like the sheep, separated from the goats, because we love God by practically loving others with sustenance, lodging, clothing, health-care and friendship?

Preparation for life in the future kingdom of heaven involves:

- Knowing Christ, the king.
- Trusting him to be true to his character of love, grace and justice.
- Humbly using the gifts He has graced us with for his kingdom.
- Patiently enduring.
- Practically loving others.

It is living out the kingdom now!

The gospel of the kingdom summarised

In summary, we can conclude from the teaching and practice of Jesus the following:

Jesus is the Messiah, the king of the kingdom of heaven.

The kingdom of heaven is where the will of the king is practised faithfully.

By seeking to do the will of the Father and doing it to its completion on the cross, Jesus fulfilled his calling of ushering in and enabling the kingdom to be realised.

The coming in of the kingdom is not done by military or political action.

The coming of the kingdom begins with repentance – turning from the rebellion of doing your own thing and by submitting to the will and ethics of the King.

It is an inside-out kingdom. It starts on the inside and is worked out in action.

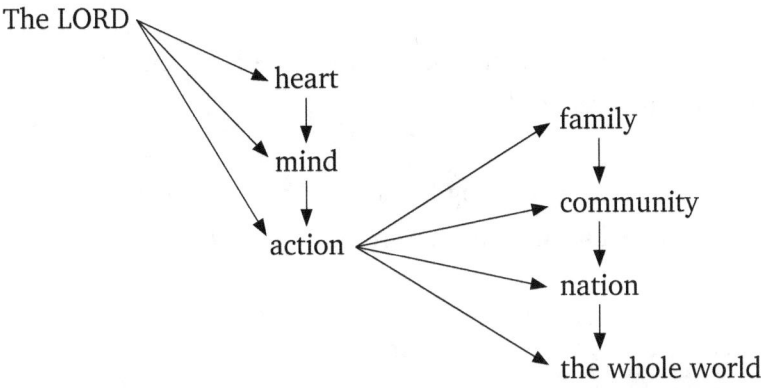

It is not realised by slavish rule-keeping and judgmentalism.

The first inside transformation is being born of the Spirit, being born from above.

The kingdom is first worked out in attitudes of humility, meekness, desiring to be righteous and to do righteously.

It is then realised through action of sacrificial love and service.

It can be worked out in all areas of our lives – in family, local community, business, practical work, political service, international service, etc.

It is an upside-down kingdom. The greatest and most effective in the kingdom will be the servant of all, doing the will of the King. The first shall be last and the last shall be first.

Our role is to seek the kingdom of God and obey the King's call to serve.

In God's time, and by God's power, the kingdom of heaven will be fully realised.

It could be said, the kingdom of God is God's cosmic conspiracy that He has announced through Jesus Christ.

REFLECTIONS

Reading the gospels, Matthew, Mark, Luke and John with the kingdom of God/heaven in mind is a great way to gain insight into the nature of the kingdom and how to live in it.

The different kingdom:

In what ways is the kingdom of heaven different to the kingdoms of this world?

How is it upside-down? How is it inside-out?

Some have said it is a 'cruciform' kingdom. What do you think that means?

Joining the kingdom:

How do we enter the kingdom of heaven?

Have you entered the kingdom of heaven? If not, now is good!

Serving the kingdom:

As you work out in this life your role in the kingdom, what attitudes can you make a deliberate attempt to adopt?

In what specific spheres of activity can you work out the principles of the kingdom at this time in your life?

7

IDENTIFYING AND FIXING THE PROBLEM

In this chapter we move on to examine some relevant teaching in the New Testament epistles.

Modern governments find themselves addressing a wide range of societal dynamics. To provide a positive context in which people can thrive, governments need to first have an accurate understanding of the foundational nature of the challenges they address. In particular, they need to identify the cause of the problems and discern what their role is in addressing them.

Identifying the problem

The problem of unrighteousness
With the inclusion of believing Gentiles in the kingdom of God, the message of the scriptures needed to be explained to them. The Hebrew scriptures, the Old Testament, describe the need for human government, God's pattern for human government,

and the relationship between righteousness and unrighteousness of the people and the nature of the government God gives them.

In his epistle to the believers in Rome, the seat of power of the empire, the apostle Paul, who had not yet been to Rome, outlines the gospel he preached. After introducing himself, he begins by defining the problem facing the whole of humanity (Romans 1:18-32).

> The wrath of God is being revealed from heaven against all the ungodliness and wickedness [unrighteousness] of people, who suppress the truth by their wickedness [unrighteousness]... (Romans 1:18)

Paul speaks of the multitude of problems in human society as the wrath of God because things have gone wrong. The Sovereign LORD created everything that is. It is subject to consistent principles. If those principles are violated, there are built-in consequences. We humans have violated His design for us and brought upon ourselves massive problems. These consequences reflect His holy integrity. His wrath is not random anger that is inconsistent with His love. His love demands that He follows the truth through to its proper consequences, without favouritism. This is justice. Ignoring sin or the withdrawal of consequences is not love. Loving justice demands experiencing consequences. The ensuing verses repeatedly say "God gave them over" to the consequences of their sin.

In saying, "the wrath of God is 'revealed' from heaven", Paul implied that a true understanding of the problem is gained through God's revelation, and that the core problem is spiritual in nature.

The existence and complexity of nature logically demands a creator. The whole of nature clearly declares the sovereign power and character of God. If the creator/sustainer God exists, we should be thankful to Him. Ingratitude is at the heart of rebellion. Logic demands we give Him glory and be accountable to Him. Humans bent on unrighteousness do not want to face this accountability and so, as Paul expresses it, we suppress this truth.

This passage in Romans 1 goes on to explain that, like Adam, humans have decided they can choose for themselves what is right and wrong, what is good and evil. To justify their defiance of God, which has become their purpose for living, they have imagined ways of celebrating and even worshipping this self-gratification. Ancient gods were personifications of not only physical aspects of nature but also of human self-gratifying attitudes and behaviour. For example, there were ancient gods of sexual lust and war. Paul lists a host of ways in which this wickedness is expressed – ways such as greed, ingratitude, unnatural self-indulgent sexual relations, depravity, envy, murder, strife, deceit, malice, gossiping, slandering, God-hating, insolence, arrogance, inventive ways of doing evil, disobeying parents, lack of understanding, and lack of fidelity, love and mercy.

When we, who live in the 'post-Christian' Western world, read this description of society we respond with, "Yes, that's what the world has come to!" The reality is the world came to this in the days of the story of Genesis, beginning with the times of Cain, Nimrod, Noah, Babel and the Canaanites, and it is much of the story of humanity ever since. The slippery slide of sin (and its consequences) is not new. Without the intervention of God, human history repeats itself.

> What has been will be again,
> What has been done will be done again;
> There is nothing new under the sun.
> Is there anything of which one can say,
> "Look, this is something new"?
> It was here long ago;
> It was here before our time. (Ecclesiastes 1:9-10)

Without the creative power of God everything is winding down. The human cosmos, the socio-political life of humanity is caught up in this vortex, following 'mother earth' into the nothingness. But God has intervened in human history, because of His great love for us, and He will continue to do so!

As explained in the earlier, it was this unrighteous state of society that necessitated civil government. Whether it be authoritarian dictatorship, the administration of a law code, or some other disciplinary control, God raises up governments and these governments have the effect of curbing the trend toward outright violent anarchy. It is a mechanism of God to restrain, but not eliminate, the worst effects of sin.

This passage in Romans 1 clearly identifies the source of the problems that governments address. The root cause of the problem is not the social-political structures present in society. The root cause is rejecting the sovereignty of God. It is failing to appreciate His power. It is ingratitude. It is failing to revere His character, in the image of which we were created. The root cause is spiritual. It is sin.

In a recent political debate on television, a group of party leaders were asked the simple question, "In your opinion, what causes crime?" Without hesitation most of them answered, "poverty". Only one had a different answer. He said, "criminal intent". I believe he was the closest to the truth. There is a significant correlation between criminal activity and poverty, but correlation is not necessarily cause and effect. Crime and poverty may well have the same root cause.

According to the Bible, social problems are a result of intent to sin in the community. People commit crime out of selfish intent. Their personal desire for something motivates them. This desire may be for power. It may be for acceptance and reputation within the group (or gang) they are in. It may be to relieve hurt or anxiety, or for social revenge. It may be for money or material goods. This desire has little or no regard for the rights or the need of someone else, the victim.

People are trapped in poverty because of someone's selfish intent. The love of money is a form of selfish intent, and it is the root cause of all kinds of evil outcomes (see 1 Timothy 6:6-10). Financial selfish intent may not be worked out with any victims in mind. It may be worked out by exploiting the system for selfish gain. Inevitably, someone is hurt. It may be worked out by deliberate crime such as theft. It may be worked out by self-indulgence which deprives someone close, such as children, of their needs. This root cause, this selfish intent, is called sin.

The consequences of denying the root problem

During the Middle Ages, Europe was ruled by various princes, dukes, kings and ruling classes. Most of these kings were independent of any accountability. There were some notable exceptions, like the legendary King Alfred the Great, who recognised his accountability to God. He based the laws of his realm on the law of God – the Ten Commandments and the Law of Love. He applied them not only to the people but also to himself. He knew that he, like all the people, was a sinner who needed the curbing of civil authority, and so subjected himself to his own laws.

Some of these medieval kings sought the approval of the Pope with the intent that they might be deemed to be the 'Holy Roman Emperor'. Clearly, to exercise authority, the official institutionalised church had resorted to the methods of the kingdoms of this world. Social control was achieved by instilling in the people the fear of the fire of hell. The sin of disobeying the rules and rites of the church would be punished in this life and in the life to come. At the time of the Reformation, the false teaching and practice of the church was exposed. Protestant leaders, representatives of the inside-out kingdom of God, were a threat to these earthly kingdoms. For example, with the backing of the official church, Louis XIV of France eliminated thousands of Protestants. Consequently, ensuing generations of the French people were mostly denied hearing the revelation of God's Word. In the 18th century, France was dominated by the church-endorsed kings and the ruling classes, the aristocracy. Aristocrats were free to do as they pleased while the peasants were effectively living in the subservience of poverty.

It was in this context there arose an intellectual movement which was to be called the Enlightenment. It was led by men such as John Locke and Jean-Jacques Rousseau. Its basic tenets applicable to civil government were:

- God was an idea not a real being, or at best was the creator influence that has 'retired' from reality and hence has not spoken. The Bible is not the revelation of God. This theology is known as Deism.
- We know by reason and observation, not by superstition under the guise of revelation. Hence this time was called the Age of Reason.
- There is no such thing as sin.
- The problem facing society is the gross injustice and inequity imposed by the ruling classes.
- If there is no such thing as sin, an egalitarian society once established by nature and social contract can rule itself.

A significant part of Enlightenment thinkers' worldview was their understanding of good and evil, right and wrong. If God was not recognised, then there was a denial of what He says is right and wrong. Therefore, they deducted that the problem they faced was not sin seated in the human heart, but the socio-political system. If the problem was the system, then the answer, their version of salvation, could be achieved by the removal of the social system. The belief was that the removal of the religious and political oppression would bring about a fair, free and happy society. Human society would be perfected. A social revolution promised to fix the problem – a political solution to solve a fundamentally spiritual problem.

This thinking under the banner of liberty, equality and fraternity (Christian values that they in ignorance took as self-evident) was behind the French Revolution. It ousted the aristocracy and led to the subsequent 'massacre' and 'reign of terror' in which anyone associated with the aristocracy was eliminated by the guillotine. The severity of the loss of life and liberty that was unleashed seemed to be worse than the injustice that previously oppressed the people. Denial of sin as the core problem gave sin an open door to express itself. In the years to follow, social control would be restored by the rise of a new warrior king and dictator, Napoleon Bonaparte. Then he too had to be exiled!

Currently, there is much discussion about the amazing potential of artificial intelligence and whether it is enabling more good or more evil. The introduction of the internet was accompanied by a similar discussion. Some envisioned a utopia that would result from the extremely enhanced ability to communicate worldwide. They thought that with the increased communication we would better be able to understand each other and work together for global common good. The net result of the use of the internet has not been the eradication of social problems. Problems still exist and their effect is actually amplified, because the source of the problems is not social structures or mechanisms but the internal selfishness, the sin of people.

Denial of sin allows it to be worked out in horrendous ways. History has many examples of tyrannical and often violent governments following revolutions fueled by the idea that the core problem is the socio-political system. For example, Marxist philosophy asserts that the core problem is the 'capitalist' system which allows the ownership of private property or capital, and the resulting inequity. In the twentieth century, many millions suffered and died during communist revolutions and their subsequent regimes.

Political saviours usually attempt to 'save' society by compulsion and suppression – because that's what governments do! It appears that God permits such governments where they are needed, to contain the effects of the sin of the people. Tyranny, with all the personal suffering that comes with it, may often be part of the "wrath of God against the godlessness and wickedness of people". As explained later in this book, the easing back of authoritarian government, such as we have experienced in 'the free world', is an outworking of God's grace.

Political revolution tempered by biblical truth

On the other side of the Atlantic Ocean, at a similar time as the French Revolution was brewing, another revolution was happening. The colonies in America were struggling with the difficulty of being subjected to the laws being shaped thousands of miles away by the British crown and parliament. After the War of Independence, there was not the equivalent of the reign of terror and a subsequent dictatorial rule. A most significant difference was that most of the people of the colonies were protestant Christians. Many of these colonies were established by people who had escaped the oppressive control of the European countries they had come from. They had escaped from oppression because of their non-conformity to religious laws. They believed in accountability to a higher authority, God. They believed in the reality of the sin of all people. For some time many had been thinking about how a Christian nation would be constituted. The ideas and outworking of the political changes in Britain, such as the bloodless revolution, in which power was transferred from the king to parliament, were in their minds. And so, in a relatively short period of time, they were able to devise the constitution of the United States of America.

The constitution of their 'republic' had built into it safeguards to counter the potential sinful inclinations of those in leadership. For example, the three arms of government, the legislative, the administration and the judicial, acted as a check on each other's power. Some subsequent refinements to the constitution further curbed the power of the state. Even as recent as the middle of the twentieth century, to counter the lust for power, the term of office of a president was limited to two four-year terms.

Most of the 'founding fathers' understood that God had established in humans, created in His image, fundamental rights – life, liberty and the pursuit of happiness. There were some who followed Enlightenment thought. For example, Benjamin Franklin was a deist. He made a last-minute amendment to the preamble of the constitution, namely that these rights were 'self-evident' rather than 'sacred'. But these rights were not self-evident to the people of much of the world. They were not self-evident to the people of the Greco-Roman world in which Christianity arose. The right to life, liberty and happiness of black skinned people was not self-evident to most of the people of America at the time when this was declared. These early American deists wanted to believe that correct structures and practices, which future generations would come to loosely call 'democracy', would 'save' the nation from the evils stemming from systemic oppression. However, Franklin and other deists like John Adams had to admit that it was the righteousness preached from the pulpits that held this delicate system together.

In times when people drifted away from God and scriptural principles and values, the nation would face internal troubles that challenged their unity and freedom. An eminent example of this, about 80 years after the establishment of the republic, was the conflict of the Civil War. The main issues at hand at this time were:

- the dynamics of centralisation of power in the federation versus the independent power of the states, and
- the issue of slavery, the failure of many to recognise the value of all human life as made in God's image regardless of 'race'.

In this scenario we observe the struggle to find a political solution to a deeper problem – that of unrighteousness.

Human rights are established not by governments but by God. Politicians would do well to look at the values, the human rights and responsibilities behind the Ten Commandments, because it is the violation of these that leads to all kinds of social problems. These values include the value of family commitment, the value of all human life, the value of ownership (or stewardship) of property, the value of telling the truth, the value of work and rest, the value of honouring agreements, and the value of contentment rather than greed. The crime of murder comes from the violation of the value of human life, the right to life. The crime of theft is the violation of the value of property rights, the right and responsibility of stewarding the things that we have in our possession. The injustice of employment exploitation comes from the violation of the value of work and rest, and from disrespecting employees created in the image of God. And all these values are built on the priority of knowing, loving and obeying God. The problems of social disconnectedness, injustice and poverty persist in all human societies. People have violated some or all of these values. Someone has sinned.

We do well to recognise that the challenges faced by society emerge directly from the heart of all the people. The problem is unrighteousness – unrighteous intent, unrighteous thinking and unrighteous practice. Understanding the heart of the problem is the first step towards finding the solution.

Fixing the problem

Having described the problem of unrighteousness in human society and having identified its root cause, being the rejection of God, the apostle Paul then describes human attempts to correct unrighteousness, to solve the problem.

Fixing the problem by judging? (Romans 2:1-11)

Sometimes we endeavour to fix the problem by judging others.

God created us to be morally accountable. It is a human trait to have a sense of what is right and wrong, and to expect others to live up to our standards of right and wrong. It is a trait of sinful humanity to pass judgement on those who don't, by telling them that they are wrong. We, who believe we know God's standards of good and evil and aspire to do His will, need to step back from this judgmental response and examine ourselves carefully. We do not have the right to pass judgement on those who do not know Him. God is judge, not us. They may well not live according to God's standards, but we do not live up to them either. Remember, Jesus warned us not to judge lest we are, in like manner, judged. Yes, we need to be discerning when observing the behaviour of others, but you and I have no right to usurp God's role of Judge. God, who knows everyone's heart, will execute just judgement in His time.

Jesus told the parables of the lost sheep, the lost coin and the lost son to religious people who were muttering judgmentalism about the people with whom Jesus associated (Luke chapter 15). With this in mind, the parable of the prodigal son would be better called the parable of the judgmental brother. Judgmental criticism does not fix the problem of unrighteousness. It does not lead to salvation.

We have heard of people who have seen the wrong lifestyle of others and have told them in no uncertain terms that they are sinners destined to hell. Such comments are interpreted as disrespect, hatred and anger. The 'sinners' have usually responded by strengthening their resolve to reject Christianity. Judgmentalism does not lead to transformation to righteousness.

> My dear brothers and sisters, take note of this: Everyone should be quick to listen, slow to speak and slow to become angry, because human anger does not produce the righteousness that God desires. (James 1:19-20)

Sadly, over the centuries, far too many Christian communities have used the power of the state to outwork judgmentalism. People with ideas that differed from the dominant community have been persecuted and killed in the name of the church or in the name of Christ. This is not the work of the kingdom of God! This is 'cancel culture' at its worst! We must let the Sovereign LORD be the judge in His time!

Fixing the problem by knowing and doing what is right? (Romans 2:12-16 and Romans 2:17-3:8)

Sometimes we think the solution is just a matter of education, knowing what is wrong and right.

God's law educates us as to what is right and wrong, but God judges us not on what we know, but on what we have done with what we know. Knowing what is right and doing it are two different things!

Most people have not been educated in the revelation of God's law. In Paul's time this was most of the Gentiles. But they do have some understanding of what is right and wrong and may sincerely attempt (or not) to live by that. Each person is accountable to God's judgement for what they have done with that understanding in their conscience.

In Romans 2, Paul then outlines the advantage of being a Jew rather than a Gentile. Jews had the law of Moses. They knew there was a holy standard. They had a measure against which to line up their own behaviour, and, if they were honest with themselves, they would know that they had failed to achieve righteousness despite striving to fulfil the law.

Paul continues, asserting that to be truly a member of Israel requires more than a life of striving to obey all the rules of the law. Such a person does not have a superior relationship to God. As much as they try, they still manage to break the law. Gentiles can see this, and the name of God is in disrepute. Truly, keeping the law involves more than outward actions observable by others. It involves an inward commitment to God. It requires firstly an inward transformation in relationship to God. This is the nature of the coming of the kingdom of God as taught by Jesus (See Luke 17:20-21). Only by internal transformation, not directly seen by physical observation, can we enter the kingdom of heaven.

As noted in the previous chapter, living in the kingdom is not a matter of, "Show me the rules and I will obey", but rather, "Show me the king and I will follow in relationship with Him".

God's purpose in giving the law through Moses was not to enable the achievement of righteousness, but rather to educate the recipients of the law, the people of Israel. It taught them that:

- God has a standard of living that they were created to follow.
- They, by their efforts to achieve righteousness, would discover how miserably short of that standard they fall.

Doing what is right is important, but it does not fix the root cause of the problem.

Fixing the problem by legislation? (Romans 3:9-20)

For some, the way to fix a problem is to legislate. The idea behind it is we can achieve goodness and hence the good life by legal coercion.

Leading up to an election in New Zealand some years ago, a political party campaigned using the slogan, "Can we fix it? Yes, we can!" That party did not become the government and so were unable to prove to everyone that – they couldn't!

It is so easy to look to the government to fix the problems we face in society. When we see the unrighteousness of social injustice, cultural conflict, violence, theft, abuse, exploitation, and dishonesty, we are disposed to look to government, through legislation and regulation, to fix it. We easily say, "The government should fix it!" We look to some political saviour. Politicians are prone to blame the present government for the problems the nation faces, and promise to fix it all when they are in power. Then, when they are in power, they don't fix everything (because they can't), and the people blame them for breaking their promises.

As Paul explains in Romans 2 and 3, the law of Moses educated the people of Israel that they needed to be saved from sin, but it did not achieve that salvation. He concluded:

> ...no one will be declared righteous in God's sight by the works of the law; rather through the law we become conscious of our sin. (Romans 3:20)

If righteousness cannot be achieved by the application of the God inspired law of Israel outlined in scripture, how much less will the application of the imperfect laws of our nation be able to fix the problems, to achieve righteousness? Whether our laws are informed to some degree by the law of God or not, the law is ineffective in achieving real righteousness.

The law alone will not bring about righteousness (social and spiritual justice). The law can make people aware of their sin and penalise them for it. Government can help reduce the consequences of rampant sin. Good laws can contribute toward the shaping of good behavioural ethics. But as a socio-political structure, government cannot eliminate the problems that plague society when those problems ultimately stem from, not the socio-political system, but the wrong motivations, the unrighteousness, the sin of the citizens.

The state is not the agent of salvation. The best political leader with the best policies and practices will not save the nation. As the Psalmist wrote:

> Do not put your trust in princes,
> in human beings who cannot save.
> When their spirit departs, they return to the ground;

> on that very day their plans come to nothing.
> Blessed are those whose help is in the God of Jacob,
> whose hope is in the LORD their God…
> He upholds the cause of the oppressed
> and gives food to the hungry.
> The LORD sets the prisoner free,
> The Lord gives sight to the blind,
> the LORD lifts up those who are bowed down,
> the LORD loves the righteous… (Psalm 146:2-9)

Paul concludes that we are all under the power of sin. Whether we think we are better than others, whether we know the law or not, whether we are Jews or Gentiles, we all are accountable to God and we all fail to achieve righteousness for ourselves or for others. There has to be a better way!

Fixing the problem God's way (Romans 3:21-31)
God can fix it, with our acceptance of His way and our cooperation with Him.

> But now apart from the law the righteousness of God has been made known, to which the law and the prophets testify. This righteousness is given through the faithfulness of Jesus Christ to all who believe. (Romans 3:21-22)

The righteousness of fulfilling God's law is achieved by the work of Christ. He achieved righteousness on our behalf. It is a gift for us to accept and then work out in relationship with Him. Our role is to trust Him and obey Him!

> Therefore, since we have been justified through faith, we have peace with God through our Lord Jesus Christ. (Romans 5:1)

The Prince of Peace has worked His reconciliation. The first effect of the work of Christ is a restored relationship with God. This restored relationship is then worked out in our relationship with one another, as Paul says about Jews and Gentiles:

> But now in Christ Jesus you who were far away have been brought near by the blood of Christ. For he himself is our peace, who has made the two groups one and has destroyed the barrier, the dividing wall of hostility. (Ephesians 2:13-14)

You don't have to be of the same ethnicity to love one another. You don't have to be of similar age to love one another. You don't have to be in the same political party to love one another. But you do have to have some sense of common connection for that love to be mutual. We can value each other if we share an understanding that we are created in the image of God. Shared reconciliation with God can have profound political consequences, within and between nations. It is a brotherhood achieved by the work of Christ and the Holy Spirit. It is a very Christian thing to be able to love those who disagree with you on significant issues.

Complete righteousness – right being, relating, doing and dealing with one another – is achieved through the work of Christ. It is not our role to achieve justice. Rather, God in

Christ has already achieved justice. Our role, as ones who are made just by the work of Christ, is to be who God has made us. We live it out, by faith in the just work of Christ, by listening to and being moved by the Spirit, and by the power of love.

REFLECTIONS

Talk that sounds judgmental:

When telling the people of the world about sin and its consequences, some single out specific sins as the root problem.

How do people read this way of talking about sin?

How can we avoid our talking about sin being interpreted as judgmentalism?

How did the apostle Paul, as recorded in Acts 17:16-33, tell the people about their sin?

Legislating morality:

Legislation is someone's moral standards put into law, but we sometimes hear this statement: "You cannot legislate morality."

What is meant by this statement?

How could the idea behind this statement be better expressed? (Think about using the word righteousness.)

Achieving righteousness:

Revisit the description of righteousness in the beginning of chapter 4. Then consider the idea of achieving the righteousness of social justice the 'inside-out' way.

What would this look like?

Discuss this statement: "Righteousness must start with the heart, but it must not stop there!"

8

THE ROLE OF GOVERNMENT

What is the role of civil government?

If the role of civil government and legislation is not to fix the problem of unrighteousness, what is its role?

In the latter part of the epistle to the Roman Christians, Paul gives practical ways to outwork our righteousness in daily living – in 'right doing' and 'right dealing'. At the beginning of chapter 13 he instructs his readers about their relationship to government.

> Let everyone be subject to governing authorities...
> (Romans 13:1)

Why should they and we be subject to authorities that are unsympathetic to the knowledge of God and at times antagonistic and adversarial to God's cause? He goes on to explain:

> ...for there is no authority except that which God has established. The authorities that exist have been estab-

lished by God. Consequently, whoever rebels against the authority is rebelling against what God has instituted, and those who do so will bring judgement on themselves. For rulers hold no terror for those who do right, but for those who do wrong. Do you want to be free from the one in authority? Then do what is right and you will be commended. For the one in authority is God's servant for your good. But if you do wrong, be afraid, for rulers do not bear the sword for no reason. They are God's servants, agents of wrath to bring punishment on the wrongdoer... (Romans 13:1-5)

From this it is clear that civil government serves God's purposes. Government controls are ordained by God to mitigate the effects of the sin which would otherwise be rampant in our fallen world.

It is also clear that we are not told to obey earthly authorities when they command us to do wrong or forbid us to do right. Obeying the higher authority of God clearly takes priority! In Acts 4, Peter pointed out to those who had arrested him and John that they were being called to account for doing an act of kindness, doing good. Then, when the officials ordered them to refrain from speaking about Jesus, Peter and John said: "Which is right in God's eyes: to listen to you, or to Him?" (Acts 4:19). Civil disobedience will incur the wrath of the civil authority. But this is far preferable to the alternative, disobeying God.

There are two functions of government mentioned in Romans 13:

- commending those who do what is right, and
- bringing punishment on those who do wrong.

Peter also refers to this as the purpose of governing authorities:

Submit yourselves for the LORD's sake to every human authority: whether to the emperor, as the supreme authority, or to governors, who are sent by Him to punish those who do wrong and to commend those who do right. (1 Peter 2:14)

These passages do not assert that these are the only legitimate functions of government, but because they are clearly identified, it is reasonable to think these are at least God's intended core functions of government. Simply put, the methodology of civil government is some kind of reward in response to the outward manifestation of righteousness – doing good, and punishment for unrighteousness – doing evil.

In both cases, it is a government's response to actions that can be observed. Governments cannot directly observe people's attitudes and motives, although in many cases the intent can be indirectly discerned. Sometimes good deeds are done for the wrong reasons, but agents of the government may not be able to tell this. The best civil government is merely a 'kingdom' of this world that can only observe and attempt to control outward behaviour.

Firstly, in response to evil doing, civic leadership can command and control. This is the domain of law and order.

Secondly, in relation to doing good, civic leadership can inspire and enable good to be done. This is working in the domain of social, economic and physical infrastructure.

Mirroring the system set up in the law of Moses, many modern free nations have three branches of government, to carry out these functions:

- Legislation – the law-making branch of government. Generally, this is a parliament or congress.
- Arbitration or Judgment – the judicial branch of government. In modern countries this is the police, law courts and penal system (see Deuteronomy 16:18-20 and Deuteronomy 17:8-13).
- Administration – the various branches of the public service, under the leadership of the government of the day.

What does punishing those who do wrong look like?
Law and order, the bringing of offenders to accountability, has been a basic function of government from the beginning. As expressed in the earlier part of this book, Genesis chapter 9 signals the need for accountability, indicating the origin of this function of government. This law and order, that civil government provides, is necessary because we live in a broken world – we are all sinners. Clearly it is the role of the government to defend the citizens from the enemy within and without the nation.

Effective law and order will not eliminate the sins we call crime. For example, laws against murder, even with very severe punishments, have existed for millennia. Murder still occurs. But where effective deterrents exist the occurrence of the crime may be less frequent. Governments can mitigate the effects of sin but cannot eliminate sin.

Some recent discussion in political circles has questioned this punitive function of government. We hear it said that 'time in jail' does not work. The assumption behind these ideas is that the purpose of the government's response to wrong-doing is to fix the wrong-doer so that they don't do it again. The question some will then ask is: Is it the purpose of the justice system to heal the offender? Is the state the agent of salvation? It certainly is the role of good government to inspire and facilitate the doing of good. What should this look like? Should the government reward counsellors and educators who work with convicted and potential criminals? This makes for lively discussion amongst policy makers.

Politicians often discuss policies related to the severity of punishments. Some insist that more severe penalties are greater deterrents. Often the factors of the swiftness and the certainty of the punishment are overlooked. Another question that could be asked is: "Should prison be the regular form of punishment?" In the law of Moses, the only 'jail' was remand in a city of refuge until there was proper judgement concerning the person's guilt or innocence and consequent action, the sentencing.

Whatever way these details are worked out, we know that when it comes to doing wrong, the role of the state is:

- to command – that is legislation, and

- to control – that is the enforcement of that legislation.

Clearly, when needed, governments should back up their authority with coercion. This must be within their circumscribed purpose – to protect and preserve the good of the people. Such coercion is illegitimate and evil when it is used to promote the governing official's own power and prestige.

What does commending those who do right look like?
To commend is to praise and encourage. Governments do well if they do not take righteous living for granted but rather encourage the people who do what is good for others.

'Doing good' has many expressions. Providing goods and services so that others can flourish is 'doing good'. Providing fulfilling employment for others is 'doing good'. Educating people so that they can flourish is 'doing good'. Caring for those who have suffered misfortune is 'doing good'. Caring for the sick and injured is 'doing good'. Good government will inspire and enable people to do good.

The government does not necessarily need to do the good themselves. Rather, it is better when the law and accompanying practice and the civic leader inspires and enables others to do good. Good governmental practice will enable, and not hinder, the doing of good. This may well involve facilitating and providing the infrastructure for people to work for the common good (flourishing) of society. Effective economic and social infrastructure enable people to do what is right. A wise government will inspire people to form stable and enduring family and community structures. They will enable parents and communities to engage suitable teachers to educate their children. It may involve rewarding the deeds of families and organisations that educate and care for others. A good government will enable doctors and health professionals to attend to those who need help to be or become healthy. An effective government will enable a person or persons with an enterprising vision to provide quality goods and services and to provide fulfilling employment for community members.

Some modern laws are designed to prevent rather than punish wrong-doing. Various licensing and compliance regulations are along this line. When these 'command and control' type rules are applied to people doing good they can become counterproductive. It is observed by some that some of these well-intended regulations are so expensive or difficult to follow through that they actually hinder, or even prevent, people from doing good. Herein is fertile ground for vigorous discussion in policy making committees!

In summary, it is God's intention that governments inspire and enable the doing of good and hinder and punish the doing of evil. The big question for us then becomes, "Does the government know what is good and what is evil?" Herein lies the great value of having political leaders and citizens who are informed by the Word of God and so understand what is truly good and what is truly evil.

The role of the good citizen

When we see something wrong in our community, or in our

nation, how do we respond? When we are made aware of or confronted with some injustice, some inequity, or some suffering, do we initially respond with: "The government should do something about it!"?

Or do we respond with, "That must be awful to experience. God, what do you want me to do about it?"

There are a whole range of possibilities of how we might be part of the answer. These include:

- Praying for the people concerned, including wrongdoers, victims and those close to them. This is the first step of action. With a listening heart, talk to the Lord about it and He can guide you to specific action.
- If the wrong is a specific illegal act, we must consider our responsibility to inform the police or other government agency of the situation.
- Practically caring for those in need.
- Introducing them to the good news of Jesus.
- Working with fellow believers to maintain ongoing support for those in need.
- Visiting prisoners, practically demonstrating the gospel in action. If we are able, helping the wrongdoers and victims through legal processes.

With the heart and skills that God has given you, there is a better way than just passing the buck to the government. Many Christians have seen a need and have prayerfully matched their skills and experience to a creative way to meet that need. Notable examples are seen in providing help, for example, with food, finance, youth training and housing.

Regard every situation as a potential opportunity. Seize the day.

> Let us not become weary in doing good... Therefore, as we have opportunity, let us do good to all people, especially to those who belong to the family of believers. (Galatians 6:9-10)

REFLECTIONS

Punishing wrongdoing:

Discuss the pros and cons of governments trying to rehabilitate wrongdoers.

Commending doing what is right:

Think about various government contexts such as health, education, immigration, welfare, law and order, taxation, etc.

What are some practical ways a government could 'commend those who do what is right'?

Do you have some creative ideas you could share with your local member of parliament?

Fixing the problems:

How can you encourage people not to always expect 'the government to fix it', and to blame the government when they don't fix it?

What opportunities are there in your community to address social problems and the needs of 'neighbours'?

What are some other things you could do?

9

CONTRASTING KINGDOMS

Knowing the difference

Before addressing the issue of believers' involvement with and in the affairs of the state, it is important to further clarify our understanding of the difference between the kingdom of heaven and the kingdoms of this world.

Earlier chapters have established the biblical concept that earthly governments are ordained by God. Their function to control is a necessity in this current fallen world. As such, they are temporary.

> For here we do not have an enduring city, but we are looking for the city that is to come. (Hebrews 13:14)

Governments which do not recognise the sovereignty of God are doomed, sooner or later, to be overthrown. Biblical prophets declare their ultimate demise. Babylon the great and all other 'Babylons', with their lust for power, their economic systems, their idolatry and exploitation of people will come crashing down at the hand of He who is Lord of all (see, for example, Isaiah 14 and 24, Daniel 2 and Revelation 16-8).

An earthly kingdom is not the opposite to the kingdom of God. The opposite of the kingdom of God is the kingdom of Satan. As the apostle Paul wrote:

> He has rescued us from the dominion of darkness and brought us into the kingdom of the Son He loves. (Colossians 1:13)

The kingdom of heaven is eternal, while earthly governments are temporal. The people involved in an earthly kingdom can be influenced by Satan and/or by God. They may be working out the principles of a spiritual kingdom – the kingdom of God for good and/or the kingdom of Satan for evil.

When Pilate was questioning Jesus about the idea that He was the king of the Jews, Jesus said:

> "My kingdom is not of this world. If it were, my servants would fight to prevent my arrest by the Jewish leaders. But now my kingdom is from another place." (John 18:36)

He did not say that His kingdom was not *in* this world, nor did He say it was not *for* this world. Jesus had already taught that the kingdom of God had come to this world. It was not just in heaven. The kingdom had come with Christ to change this world. Rather, Jesus said that His kingdom was not *of* or *from* this world. The kingdom of heaven is of a different nature to the kingdoms of the world.

In drawing this contrast between the nature and origin of kingdoms, Jesus drew attention to an important difference. The entirely different nature of the Kingdom of Heaven determined the way the servants of His Kingdom should operate in relation to a worldly kingdom. Servants of earthly kingdoms overtly 'fight' or exercise force to achieve their purposes. Understanding the different nature and outworking of the kingdom of heaven helps us, as believers, to know what to do when we live in this time when we experience these different kingdoms concurrently.

The story of human governments, the kingdoms of this world, is the story of humans attempting to achieve their earthly version of the kingdom of heaven, their 'utopia'. Political leaders often declare that they are striving to achieve the good of the people. That seems similar to the purposes of the kingdom of heaven, the glory of God and our salvation, the flourishing or shalom (peace) of humanity. To achieve this, governments often embark on measures over and above just punishing wrong and commending right. Not just benign but tyrannical regimes can claim to operate for the good of the people. For example, in the 20th century the communist regime in Russia and the Nazi regime in Germany were adamant they were pursuing the good of the people. However, an earthly kingdom is not the agent of salvation and cannot achieve such utopian goals!

In some ways, earthly kingdoms do have similarities to the heavenly, but even the best lack the crucial factor. They are kingdoms that inevitably are without God. God is left out in some, or all, of these three facets:

- Without God as Sovereign King.
- Without the Word of God informing the kingdom as to what is right and wrong.
- Without the work of the Spirit of God, transforming the people internally and empowering them to do what is right.

Without God as King

About 1600 years ago, in *The City of God*, Augustine of Hippo wrote that the earthly city glories in itself and the heavenly city glories in the LORD. When God is not revered and obeyed as sovereign, something or someone else holds the power and prestige. This may be:

- A monarch, a king or a dictator who has absolute power.
- A group, or a political party that assumes absolute power.
- Powerful controllers or influencers of the economy controlling decisions.
- Public opinion is regarded as the determiner of what is right. In this case, media influencers effectively hold the power.
- An ideology such as capitalism, communism or pragmatism.

Even attempts to give the ultimate power to the people can be a substitute for the sovereignty of God.

Yes, some of these alternatives are preferable to others, but they all can serve as alternatives to the sovereignty of God.

The revolutionaries in the late eighteenth century in France had a motto: Liberty, Equality, Fraternity. This expression of their fundamental values has continued to be part of France's national heritage and is part of the current French constitution. It has been echoed in the values of many modern nations.

From where did these values come? While the revolutionaries saw the Christianity of the establishment as the enemy, these values actually came from a biblical Christian worldview! They are radical major themes of the New Testament. The New Testament in particular taught that we are free in Christ. The Bible teaches that we are all created equally in the image of God, we are all equally culpable for our sin and equally redeemable by the work of Christ. The New Testament teaches that in Christ we are all children of God, brothers and sisters, regardless of our ethnicity or social class. We can be set free from sin and be one in Him. The Christian idea of freedom is that we are free to do what is right in God's eyes, while the world, in Adam, looks for freedom to do 'what I want', and to 'do it my way'.

In the century following the French Revolution, Western nations emphasised liberty with great zeal. For many, liberty became an idol. Then, with the rise of Christian social reform and then socialist thought, the next 100 years saw equality brought to the fore around the world. For many, equality became an idol. And so, there are political parties who tend to pursue freedom even if it is at the expense of equality and others who tend to pursue equality even if it is at the expense of freedom. It is a difference of priorities. They have been labelled left-wing or right-wing. While there has been a consciousness in the background that we ultimately are under God, there has been a reasonable respect for each other and the 'democratic' process.

The position of God in all of this is critical. If God is not seen as the ultimate authority, the dominant ideology becomes idolised. Dominant ideals may be: love of pleasure, of money, of free enterprise or free market, of free sex, of narcissism, militarism, or various other pursuits. If idolised, or absolutised they become gods with spiritual power. The epistles of the New Testament call them powers, authorities, thrones, dominions or rulers in high places. If the individualistic free market is idolised, as in 'private capitalism', the poor are subjected to the oppression of sinners with economic power. If equality in the community is idolised, as in state capitalism or communism, freedom is compromised or even destroyed by those in power.

It is refreshing when we see governmental recognition of accountability to God. In the year 2000, Queen Elizabeth II gave her Christmas message to the people of the Commonwealth, as she had been doing for many years. On this occasion she chose to address the relevance of the year 2000, noting it was 2000 years since the year of Christ (Anno Domini), the assumed year of Christ's birth. She reflected on how she had a reputation of being dutiful in her role. She said this was because she recognised that she was accountable to God, and that was why she was faithful to her calling. This humble and dutiful service was a significant reason why millions trusted her as their queen, and it was a salutary reminder to us all that God, and not the government, is truly sovereign.

The preamble to the constitution of the Commonwealth of Australia mentions the idea of the people of all the states humbly relying on the blessing of God. Indeed, one suggested preamble to the constitution at the time of federation said, "Duly acknowledging Almighty God as the supreme ruler of the universe and the source of all true government..." Sadly, that idea is rarely considered by most Australians today.

Nations like New Zealand where I live have had the tradition of opening parliamentary sessions with prayer, the idea being that parliament was accountable to God. This heritage was an expression of centuries of Christian influence on the English-speaking world. Sadly, moves have been made to remove it from customary practice in many parliaments. Where used, it is practised in a perfunctory way, as God is rarely recognised after the 'amen' has been said.

When God is no longer served, as happened at the fall and incessantly since, it makes way for the horrendous problems experienced by humanity throughout history. Joshua challenged the nation of Israel to choose whom they would serve, God or some other power. Each government and people of a nation are faced with this same choice: do they recognise God as sovereign, or do they submit to some other power or dominion?

Without the Word of God

How do we know what is true and what should guide us in our decision-making? When the Word of God is not the prime informer of right and wrong, something else, an alternative worldview becomes the foundation of our decision-making. In the past these have included:

- Dictates of the church hierarchy, assuming to be the Word of God.
- The ideas of Enlightenment philosophers and political theorists.
- The ideas of socialist philosophers, such as Karl Marx.

And in the current context these could be the absolutising of:

- Evidential empiricism – scientific observation and research as the only way to know.
- Post-modern understanding of truth and tolerance – no absolute truth only personal preference, so anything can be tolerated.
- The philosophy behind ideas such as critical race theory.
- The absolutising of freedom or liberty.
- Intransigent conservatism.

Yes, we may see truth or value in some or all of these, but they can become substitutes for the primary source of wisdom, the Word of God. All truth, if it is the truth, is God's truth.

The fear of the Lord is the beginning of wisdom,
And knowledge of the Holy One is understanding.
(Proverbs 9:10)

The Hebrew word for wisdom means more than just theoretical knowledge or internal attitude. It means knowing what to do and how to do it. True wisdom is practised knowledge.

All scripture is God breathed and is useful for teaching, rebuking, correcting and training in righteousness. (2 Timothy 3:16)

This verse in Timothy shows us that:

- Scripture can teach us what is right and wrong – teaching.
- Scripture can alert us to when we have done wrong – rebuking.
- Scripture can lead us to put right what we have done – correcting.
- Scripture can nurture or train us to get it right in the future – training in righteousness.

Not only individuals, but governments would do well to heed this advice and consult the Word of God. Without the Word of God informing their values, governments can have amazingly divergent ideas about what is right and wrong and how to correct the problems they face. Moral truth becomes a fluid thing! What is evil in the eyes of some can be determined to be good, and what is good can be determined to be evil! The net result is confusion and conflict.

Without the Spirit of God

When the exiled Jews were returning from Babylon and re-establishing their occupancy of Jerusalem, the first building project was the temple. Reinstating their rhythm of relationship with God was the first step in rebuilding the city of God. They faced severe opposition from the people already living in the land. God's word to the people of the time through the prophet Zechariah was, "Return to Me, and I will return to you" (Zechariah 1:3). The people would be blessed, and others through the work of God in them would be blessed too. To Zerubbabel, the project leader, God said, it would be achieved "not by might, nor by power, but by my Spirit" (Zechariah 4:6). The method of the kingdom of heaven is the work of the Holy Spirit.

The first chapter of the book of Acts speaks about the resurrected Christ teaching his disciples about the kingdom of God. "He appeared to them over a period of forty days and spoke about the kingdom of God." He promised that they would be baptised with the Holy Spirit. They asked Him, "Lord, are you at this time going to restore the kingdom to Israel?" He responded that it would happen in the Father's timing, "but you will receive power when the Holy Spirit comes on you: and you. will be my witnesses in Jerusalem, and in all Judea and Samaria, and to the ends of the earth." The power of the kingdom of heaven is the work of the Holy Spirit, and it affects beyond the borders of Israel (Acts 1:1-8). Jesus said about the Holy Spirit:

> When He comes, He will prove the world to be in the wrong about sin and righteousness and judgment: about sin, because people do not believe in me; about righteousness, because I am going to the Father, where you can see me no longer; and about judgment, because the prince of this world now stands condemned... But when He, the Spirit of truth, comes, He will guide you into all the truth... (John 16:8-15)

The initial role of the Spirit in the kingdom is to:

- Convict us of our wrong attitude toward the LORD.
- Convict us of our subsequential wrong ideas of what is right.
- Convict us of our erroneous assessment of what is wrong.

The Holy Spirit renews the attitudes and thinking of people. To do this, He uses His effective weapon, the Word of God, to destroy the old way of thinking and reshape the way we think about all of life. He inspires and enables us to outwork His righteousness, His love in all areas of life, including the public sphere.

Substitute methods for the work of God's Spirit in achieving social change can be:

- Legal compulsion and regulatory control.
- Fear-mongering.
- The threat of shame and the promise of prestige.
- Military enforcement.
- Financial incentives appealing to the love of money.
- Religious judgementalism and legalism.

These are methods of kingdoms of the world, and as such some of these have effectiveness, albeit limited, and may be necessary to achieve a degree of law and order. But they fall short of the ideal of the internal work of the Spirit being worked out and expressed in the fruit of the Spirit (see Galatians 5:22), and subsequential practical action.

The work of the kingdom is not being bound to following a set of biblical rules and rituals, or even biblical principles. It is an outworking of a relationship with the king, consistent with the principles of His Word, and guided and empowered by the Holy Spirit. For citizens of the kingdom, this is the modus operandi for living the whole of life. There is no 'sacred/secular' division of one's life. God is king of all of life, and all of life is to be lived in relationship with Him.

The church and the state

The distinct differences between the two types of kingdom leads us to ask whether there can be an overlap in their functions. And so, we can be led to ask these questions:

- Should we expect the governments of our nations

or cities to follow God and the principles of the Kingdom of God?
- Should we be comfortable with the institutionalised church using the methods of earthly kingdoms?

It is too simplistic to say the two kingdoms are totally different and never will they meet! Inevitably there is interaction between them and some form of 'syncretism', for better or worse, will occur.

A Christian state?

Firstly, should we expect the governments of our nations or cities to follow God and the principles of the kingdom of God? Should they enforce the principles of God's kingdom?

It is an interesting idea, but they are kingdoms of this world. They are ordained by God but are not the agents of the kingdom of God. God's people, the church, are to be the heralds of and agents of the kingdom of Christ. The state has a different role to the church.

In the 4th century, the Roman emperor Constantine caught on to the idea of bearing the sign of a cross before the army going to war. He saw that he could possibly achieve his worldly ambition of military victory by using this Christian religious symbol. His initial success caused him and his successors to adopt Christianity as the religion of the Roman Empire. The nature of Constantine's conversion is debated. It is not our role to judge, but we can appreciate that this opened up the door for massive changes. Political leaders were open to listening to the church and the church was influenced by the political leadership. Thus began the working out of a complex relationship between the church and the state over the next millennium or so.

As the Roman Empire declined, the church leadership, headed up by the bishop of Rome, the Pope, assumed more political power. In the 5th century, Augustine of Hippo wrote a pivotal work entitled *The City of God* to speak into this situation. He presented human history as a metaphysical conflict between the earthly city inspired by Satan and the heavenly city, the people of God.

The Roman Empire became divided into east and west and then further divided into many local kingdoms. While influenced by the ideas and values of Christianity, they were still kingdoms of this world doing what kingdoms of this world do. A mix of ideas stemming from Christianity influenced these political powers. Sometimes a king would actively promote Christianity. A notable example was Charlemagne, a king of the Franks, who expanded his kingdom and made considerable reforms in administration, law and education in line with his religious commitment. In 800, he was endorsed by the Pope as the Emperor and became the forerunner of a line of Holy Roman Emperors. Europe came to be called Christendom.

In the south they had to resist the military invasion of Islam. In response, military crusades to capture the land of Israel and Jerusalem were instigated or supported by the popes. Wars between the kingdoms were often given Christian justification. Christendom was effectively a Christian religious kingdom or cooperation of kingdoms, nothing like the kingdom of heaven. They were kingdoms of this world. Subsequently, Christianity was used by these kingdoms as a tool or a justification to invade and colonise the new world, the Americas, the east and the south.

In our current 'post-Christian' world, the leaders of earthly kingdoms are mostly not informed by the Word of God, and they are leading a people that are largely not remotely inclined to listen to God's Word or the Holy Spirit. And so, even if the political leaders believe in God and recognise accountability to Him, to achieve some degree of social order or social change, they will need to use alternative methods to that of the Spirit. As we have discussed before, civil governments will use some form of coercion, reward and punishment – commend those who do what is right and bring punishment on those who do wrong. This is right and what they should do, but this is not the method of the kingdom of heaven.

Change achieved by mere human effort is not permanent. Changes in the law and the political system will only endure until someone in the future reverses or undoes the change. History has the habit of repeating itself. Indeed, change can often be an illusion of progress.

Social progress or improvement is a relatively modern concept, probably derived from many generations engaging with the idea of improvement achieved through the work of Christ. Only God can work permanent improvement.

A coercive church?

Secondly, should we be comfortable with the institutional church using the methods of earthly kingdoms?

Governments and their various departments are agents of

earthly kingdoms, while the church, the people of Christ with their various organisational and ritual expressions, are the agents of the kingdom of heaven.

This is not the place to explore the doctrine of the church, but rather briefly visit the relationship between the church and state. The story of the early church unfolded when there was no idea of the state and the church conducting similar business. State authorities had their God-ordained role while the church was called to proclaim, in word and deed, the good news of Jesus Christ and His different type of kingdom. There was no expectation that the church should organise itself like an earthly kingdom with hierarchical leadership and a head of state. As the epistles taught, Christ is the head and we each are part of the body subject to the headship of Christ (See 1 Corinthians 3). Nor was there any idea in the New Testament that the church would practise its ethics by law enforcement. In fact, the New Testament writers vehemently spoke against 'legalism'.

In the centuries following the Roman Empire accepting Christianity and the subsequent collapse of the empire, the church began to take on political power and forms and methods of government that were characteristic of earthly kingdoms. It seemed like the spiritual kingdom of God had got lost in the milieu of the prevailing kingdoms. However, some had access to the Word of God and in every generation examples of real faith in Christ existed within the formal church or in organisations parallel to the church. For example, the life of many monks in medieval times was a genuine expression of the work of the kingdom of God. The word 'secular' was used to describe these monastic ministries. 'Secular' meant separate from the control of the institutional church.

During this time there were some voices questioning the use of coercion to promote the kingdom of God. For example, in the 800s, the monk, Alcuin of York, who was an advisor to the Holy Roman Emperor, Charlemagne, was a radical voice. He urged the Emperor to stop forcing pagans to be baptised or be killed. He said in one of his advisory letters something to this effect: Faith is a free act of the will, not a forced act. We must appeal to the conscience, not compel it by violence. You can force people to be baptised, but you cannot force them to believe.

Even when foundational truths of the Bible, such as justification by faith, were rediscovered in the Reformation, protestant groups which broke away from the governmental authority of the Roman Church, still perpetuated some of the methods of the state within their church communities. For example, some attempted to control the state to achieve the work of the kingdom of heaven. Others used the power of the sword to eliminate heresy.

It is only 300 years ago that, in the West, the separation of the institutional church and the state was again considered! It was proposed that the state was to be 'secular' in that it was not under the control of the church, and the teaching and functions of the church were not controlled by the state. Some people of the USA, notably, took a lead in this. The state was to listen to the 'prophetic' voice of the church and practise righteousness, rather than be controlled by the church.

Since that time, particularly in recent decades, there has been an increasing rejection of any expression of Christianity in public life, so that separation of church and state has now come to mean the removal of Christian ideas from the affairs of the state. The word 'secular' has come to mean totally non-religious. The state has resisted more and more the influence of the church, to the point where many think that Christianity is an irrelevant sideshow.

Meanwhile, within the church, the people of the kingdom of heaven, there have been various ways of coordinating operations, using a range of models of church government. Indeed, some denominations gained their names from their method of church government, such as Episcopal, Congregational, Presbyterian, and Methodist arrangements. Each have their merits and their time and place. In the United Kingdom, where the Anglican Church still has constitutional connection with the leadership of the state, the church leaders accept this as an opportunity to speak into the places of government, and this formal connection is a timely reminder that there is ultimate accountability to God.

Alongside the institutional church, there have also been various parachurch movements and organisations which endeavour to extend the work of the kingdom of heaven. These include welfare organisations, educational institutes and schools, groups promoting a particular aspect of the Christian faith such as Christian apologetics, and organisations speaking into the governmental sphere, the public square. They each have their way of functioning, according to their calling. They each require some form of official governance.

The questions we, as Christian leaders, as agents of the kingdom of God, need to ask ourselves are:

- Is the LORD regarded as sovereign, or is it something or someone else?
- Is the Word of God or some other authority guiding our action?
- Is the Spirit our enabler?

Are we operating like a kingdom of this world or as the agents of the kingdom of heaven?

These questions are particularly applicable to the leadership of the church. Leadership can so easily become chains of command and control. At a leadership conference some years ago, I remember a wise pastor of a big church in New Zealand describing his leadership style. He said that in their church they developed a 'culture of permission giving'. If someone asked him if they could initiate some activity in the church, he would reply, 'Yes. How can we help?' As a result, he said, there were numerous 'ministries' or practical services going on in and through the church. A significant proportion of the non-government welfare services in their city stemmed out of the work of this church. As the leader, he said he was learning about the details of what these groups were doing as he went along. He was asked, "How do you keep control of it all?" He replied, "Why would I want to do that? Yes, I need to observe and advise, but I am their leader, not to control, but to help them serve God and the community".

Christian leadership, whether in the church, in the community or public square, is not meant to be focused on command and control, but rather on inspiring and enabling the team to do what they are called to do. Yes, there are contexts and times when there is a need to confront and correct, but this is not the day to day mode of operation within the kingdom of God.

In this life there will always be a dynamic tension between the kingdom of God and the kingdoms of this world. In the next chapters we address the way citizens of the kingdom of heaven can interact with and in the functions of state.

REFLECTIONS

A Christian nation?

Given the contrasting nature of the kingdom of God and civil 'kingdoms', discuss the concept of a Christian nation.

Why is this considered an oxymoron by some?

In what way can a nation be considered 'Christian'?

Consider the story of the emperor Constantine adopting some Christian cultural forms.

What do you think was his motivation for doing this?

In what way did the Roman Empire become 'Christian' in the years to follow?

Effecting the kingdom:

Discuss the statement, "The kingdom of God is not achieved by human force, psychological, political or military coercion."

Investigate the methods of evangelism used by the Conquistadores in Latin America.

These were the methods of what kingdom?

What can we learn from this piece of history?

In the early 1600s, Puritan believers, in pursuit of religious freedom, left Europe and settled in America in what is now called New England. They established community structures in line with their Christian faith. How were they going to affirm righteousness? In 1646 the Massachusetts Bay Colony made it a capital offence to deny that the Bible was the Word of God.

How does this sit with your understanding of the kingdom of God and the biblical ideals about the relationship between church and state? Think about the purpose and the method of the kingdom.

In the light of the methodology of the kingdom discussed in this chapter:

Should evangelists use psychological or emotional persuasion to achieve conversions?

Up to whom should we leave the 'coercion' to convert?

10

INFILTRATING AND OVERCOMING

We find ourselves in a time where the kingdom of heaven has been established in the lives of those who recognise the King as Lord, yet the full dominion as was intended in the beginning and will be in a time to come is not yet fully realised. What difference can the kingdom of heaven have in the midst of worldly kingdoms?

In addressing this question, I have chosen Isaiah chapters 32 and 33 to frame this discussion of how the agents of the kingdom of heaven, believers between Christ's first and second coming have lived in and affected the kingdoms of the world. Isaiah 32 is foretelling the yet to come time when the kingdoms of this world have become the kingdom of God. In this chapter I attempt to describe that in the meantime, where the kingdom of God has influenced the structures of society, we have seen a limited foretaste of that which is to come.

The power of infiltration

Prophesying over 700 years before the time of Jesus Christ,

Isaiah speaks of a future kingdom. He paints a picture of the kingdom of the king who will reign in righteousness while, initially, evil is still happening in the world – the perfect restoration of all things has yet to be fully worked out.

Refuge and discernment (Isaiah 32:1-8)

> See, a king will reign in righteousness
> and rulers will rule with justice.
> Each one will be like a shelter from the wind
> and a refuge from the storm. (Isaiah 32:1-2)

Where the kingdom of God is actively present, there will be rulers who lead with righteousness and justice. In the realms where these leaders preside, the plight of the oppressed will be seen, and their cry will be heard. The knowledge of the truth will bring freedom. Free and enterprising people will confidently articulate and pursue their dreams. These realms will be places of refuge and nourishment.

> Then the eyes of those who see will no longer be
> closed, and the ears of those who hear will listen.
> The fearful heart will know and understand, and the
> stammering tongue will be fluent and clear.
> No longer will the fool be called noble nor the
> scoundrel be highly respected. (Isaiah 32:3-5)

The practice of ungodliness and the spreading of error about God will still be occurring. But fools and scoundrels with their lies and exploitation of the vulnerable will not be celebrated by the wise and noble. Rather, the wise will see them for what they are.

> Scoundrels use wicked methods, they make up evil schemes to destroy the poor with lies, even when the plea of the needy is just.
> But the noble make noble plans, and by noble deeds they stand. (Isaiah 32:7-8)

Jesus told some parables about the Kingdom of Heaven infiltrating and influencing the world. He said the Kingdom of Heaven was like yeast mixed into dough until it worked through all the dough (see Matthew 13:33). He also said the Kingdom of Heaven is like a mustard seed, tiny in the beginning but growing into the largest plant in the garden, so that birds seek refuge in its branches (see Matthew 13:31-32).

Isaiah's prophecy could well be describing the effect of the kingdom of God in those nations that have had a long history of Christian values and practices infiltrating into the fabric of the nation. In recent centuries, there have been nations where people have engaged with the truth of scripture and have worked it out into both private and public life. Biblical values have been instilled into the thinking of much of the population, even in many who do not believe in Christ as Lord. Consequently, many have flourished socially and economically. These nations have become safe havens into which a flood of refugees and immigrants come to escape the suffering and exploitation they are experiencing elsewhere. They are attracted to nations where:

- their work is valued and rewarded,
- human lives (including their women's lives) are valued,
- commitment to the truth and promise-keeping is valued,
- property rights are respected, and where
- political leaders are subject to the will of the people.

These nations have been far from perfect. They have displayed the same dispositions as other kingdoms of this world, such as imperialism, exploitation of certain economic or racial groups and the disrespect of indigenous peoples. However, the strategic influence of people of the kingdom of God has enabled these nations to progressively address these issues, albeit imperfectly. Governments that have embraced the vision of social justice have enabled the people to enjoy a comparative flourishing.

> ...rulers will rule with justice ... by noble deeds they stand. (Isaiah 32:1 & 8)

Over the centuries, the development of western nations has not been the political establishment of the kingdom of God. It has been the rise of dominions which have competed against each other for power and have extended their power through the processes of imperial colonisation and economic hegemony. These things have been characteristic of kingdoms and societies through all ages, both ancient and modern, and all regions of the earth.

But in 'the West' there has been another most significant development. There has been the progressive devolution of the power of the kings. This has been noticeable particularly in western Europe and English-speaking nations. Of course, this has nothing to do with being British or north-western European. The difference has been the engagement of people within these nations with the revelation of the Bible.

The Bible teaches that all humans are specially created by the one God, in His image. It thus promotes the prior value of human life – all human life. It promotes the idea that all people have the responsibility and privilege of making moral choices. God's pivotal command is to love Him and all other people – without prejudice. Rights and privileges are granted to all, not just leaders and their colleagues.

Most Christian political leaders from all parties have believed this. For example, Sir Robert Menzies, who was the Prime Minister of Australia for many years in the middle of last century, said:

> Democracy ... is based upon the Christian conception that there is in every human soul a spark of the divine; that, with all their inequalities of mind and body, the souls of men (humans) stand equal in the sight of God. (From: Mahlburg K, Sir Robert Menzies: Twenty Quotes on Faith and Freedom, The Daily Declaration, 24 June 2021)

Embedded in this concept of humans being the image of God, 'imago Dei', are various implications. These include concepts such as the call of God for us to work. People have the responsibility to fulfil this calling. The Bible teaches that we all, leaders and followers, are accountable to a higher authority, God Himself. The Bible teaches the value of truth and faithfulness to promises. Consequently, people with some of these ideas embedded in their psyche are capable of a degree of self-government, and the people should be allowed the opportunity to accept such responsibility. Along with the promotion of the biblical idea of the rule of law, this has led to structures which have reduced the power of kings and given more responsibility to the people.

In Britain, an early example of devolution of the power of the king was the Magna Carta. It made a big step in the removal of the power of judgement from the king to a law court separate from the royal court where judgement was made by a panel of peers, a jury. Then, came the development of a parliament which initially consisted of members of the aristocracy, but then of representatives of the common people. The 'bloodless revolution ' of 1688 made parliament effectively equal partners with the monarchy. Britain became a constitutional monarchy, where the king was not only accountable to God, but the king's powers were limited, and he was subject to the law like any other person. Meanwhile we have seen the development of republics such as the United States of America, where even the head of state, the president, is chosen by the people.

With the reduction of the threat of authoritarian rulers, the people were able to pursue innovative ideas. Some sought to think God's ideas in relation to nature, and thus discovered something of the way God rules the natural world. Thus, political freedom was one factor that enabled the rise of modern science. Others have enjoyed the freedom to develop artistic, philanthropic, clothing and food production business enterprises. Sadly, too many have used this freedom to exploit or use others to fulfil their selfish desires. This exploitation of freedoms, in turn, leads to increased regulations – a reduction in our freedoms.

In nations where there has been the devolution of the power of kings, the application of biblical principles has been very far from perfect. At times there have been attempts to achieve the kingdom of God by coercion. Some have used Christianity to justify the injustices of racism and sexism, and so it has taken many generations to work out these biblical principles into accepted societal norms. And still in many people there is a heart resistant to social justice. However, overall, there has been unprecedented freedom and flourishing of the people.

Other nations have, with varying degrees of success, copied these patterns of government. Where there is little social cohesion and where the lust for power and corruption prevail, these forms of government have been a failure. This reality leads us to ask: Is this flourishing primarily the result of the political structures in these nations, or is it the result of the ability of the people to understand the biblical values and to embrace the responsibility of self-government under God?

In the last 100 years or so, this style of political structure has been called democracy. The word democracy means rulership by the people. Possibly it is a misnomer, since these nations are ruled by representatives of the people, not the people themselves. It is often said that the West got the concept of democracy from ancient Greece. This is in part true. In some ancient Greek cities political decisions were made by the consensus of the assembly of the educated elite (at best, about 20 percent of the population), in the public forum. However, this is quite different from modern representative governments, which involve vast numbers of people in multiple cities choosing their representatives in the legislative bodies.

During the Reformation, theologian John Calvin was invited to establish a theocratic government in the city of Geneva. This attempt to syncretise kingdoms was not entirely successful. The people had to work out what biblical principles were applicable to government and what did their outworking look like. They made mistakes, but it seems they learned in the process. Geneva not only created a home base for the emerging protestant movement through Europe, but also started the application of biblical principles in the structure of government throughout Switzerland. Today Switzerland is probably the most 'democratic' nation in the world. Legislative power is decentralised, with each Canton (local region) confirming legislation by referendum. The federal government is led by a team not just one person. Over the years Switzerland has been, in many aspects of life, a safe haven, a place of refuge.

It is not universally recognised that the success of this type of political structure is beholden, not to the structure, but to the degree of righteousness or self-government of the people and their political leaders. For example, if a significant number of the population have criminal intent, the nation will need to become more of a 'police state'. If the elected leaders do not respect the rights and responsibilities of the people, the nation will become a 'dictatorship of the 51 percent'. There are numerous examples around the world of elected leaders who have gained power and then eliminated the opposition. 'Banana republics' are often a result of democratic structures being thrust onto people who do not have enough commitment to the values that sustain freedom.

Communities flourish when people of the kingdom of heaven infiltrate (like salt and yeast) into every aspect of the society. When the people reject the king and the values of the kingdom, societal order will collapse, as Isaiah's prophecy describes.

Economic security or collapse (Isaiah 32:9-20)

Addressing women luxuriating on the benefits of economic prosperity, Isaiah warns them that this feeling of security is false. In just a few months the economy would collapse. This was expressed by Jesus when he said,

> Store up for yourselves treasures in heaven, where moths and vermin do not destroy, and where thieves do not break in and steal. (Matthew 6:20)

This passage does not specifically say what causes such economic collapse, but the greater context is that of the prophet warning the people of the dire consequences of their unrighteousness. This prophecy can serve as a warning to us who live in the prosperity of the modern world. Our prosperity, with its 'democratic' structures, is very fragile and can disintegrate rapidly when we abandon the righteousness which sustains it. Various recent events, manifesting political discontent, in the free world have made us aware of political and social instability resulting from the abandonment of the values on which our nations have been built.

Isaiah pronounces that this economic woe will last until:

> the Spirit is poured on us from on high,
> and the desert becomes a fertile field. (Isaiah 32:15)

The source of this economic renewal and social prosperity will be the righteousness that comes with the Spirit. There are many examples in modern history of communities and even whole nations with serious social problems being turned around, not by government measures, but by some spiritual revival or renewal in the people. The Holy Spirit sovereignly turns hearts and consequent actions around. The 'Welsh revival' in 1904 is just one example. Thousands of working-class people turned from an undisciplined lifestyle and joined large revival meetings. The occurrence of domestic violence and crime plummeted. When police officers become redundant, something special is happening!

> The LORD's justice will dwell in the desert,
> His righteousness live in the field.
> The fruit of that righteousness will be peace;
> Its effect will be quietness and confidence forever.
> (Isaiah 32:16-17)

The result of righteousness is the peace (flourishing), quiet confidence, and security of the people.

Isaiah's description of prosperity includes peaceful and secure rural dwellings and farming. There is security beyond the protection of the city walls. Righteous citizens and just leadership provide the environment for productive, fulfilling work. This all begins with the Spirit of righteousness, the kingdom of heaven at work on earth.

The power of endurance

Help and hope in the middle of distress (Isaiah 33:1-12)
Isaiah's prophecy continues in Chapter 33. He describes the wanton destruction of destroyers who will in turn be destroyed, and of betrayers who will be betrayed. Such power struggles and war mongering are typical of the kingdoms of this world. Isaiah describes times when there is great unfaithfulness and distress. Living in this context are those who long for God, who have daily strength and hope in Him. For them, the LORD is gracious. He remains their strength, and they have the hope of His justice and His righteousness.

> LORD, be gracious to us; we long for you.
> Be our strength every morning, our salvation in times of distress. (Isaiah 33:2)

He will be a rich source of security, salvation, wisdom and knowledge.

He will be a sure foundation for your times,
a rich store of salvation and wisdom and knowledge;
the fear of the LORD is the key to this treasure.
(Isaiah 33:6)

Isaiah is describing times when the influence of the Kingdom of Heaven through His people will not be seen in the life of the nation in which they live. This is much like the experience of people living in nations that are not part of the 'free world'. But the kingdom is within their souls and communities and the lordship of Jesus will sustain them.

It was in this context of persecution by Roman and local political authorities that Jesus gave the apostle John His revelation. Revelation, the Apocalypse, is a message to believers, citizens of the kingdom of heaven, living in the context of earthly kingdoms. The political powers do not understand the nature of the kingdom of heaven and are antagonistic toward those who worship a different king, a superior sovereign Lord. In graphic picture language, Revelation depicts the spiritual forces at work in this scenario and describes the ongoing battle. At the same time as kingdoms are raging against each other and against the citizens of the kingdom of God, Christ the Lord is enthroned in heaven and the saints are worshipping Him. These saints, believers who are spiritual overcomers, are blessed while anticipating the final victory of Christ, the Lamb, the final judgement and the restoration of the earth. Heaven ultimately becomes fully established in the new earth.

The message of Revelation is clear: Those who worship the Sovereign King are overcomers. The process of overcoming is the method of the sacrificial Lamb, not that of the marauding lion. The process will often be difficult and even traumatic, but the servants of Jesus are kept and preserved, even if they lose their lives in the process. Ultimately good triumphs over evil. The Lamb will achieve victory and will be King. He will be triumphant for ever and ever. Repeatedly, the promise is made that His followers who overcome will share in His victorious rule.

Provision in the middle of anxiety (Isaiah 33:13-16)

Isaiah describes contrasting mindsets in uncertain times – fears and anxieties versus peace. The people who are far from God are gripped with terror, fearing that which is coming on the earth – the natural consequences of human sin, the wrath of God.

> You who are far away, hear what I have done;
> you who are near, acknowledge my power!
> The sinners in Zion are terrified;
> trembling grips the godless:
> "Who of us can dwell with consuming fire?
> Who of us can dwell with everlasting burning?"
> Those who walk righteously
> and speak what is right,
> who reject gain from extortion
> and keep their hands from accepting bribes,
> who stop their ears from plots of murder
> and shut their eyes against contemplating evil –
> they are the ones who will dwell on the heights,

whose refuge will be the mountain fortress.
Their bread will be supplied, and water will not
fail them. (Isaiah 33:13-16)

We live in a world characterised by anxiety. There is fear of environmental disaster, of diseases, of wars, and of social and political collapse. What a refuge is the God of the Kingdom of Heaven! What peace there is when we set our hearts and minds on the things above, not on earthly things! (See Colossians 3:1-10.) What confidence can prevail when God's people conduct their lives according to the principles of the kingdom of heaven!

Hope of a glorious future (Isaiah 33:17-24)

Isaiah continues his prophecy. He speaks of the time when the Messiah King will visibly reign on earth. When the King is seen in all His glory, in all His beauty, the people will look back and say:

- Where is the former terror?
- Where are those who are corrupt?
- Where are those who were violent?
- Where are those who scored their victories of power and prestige?
- Where are those who had deceptive speech, clever spin?

Instead, they will experience:

- The permanent presence of the LORD, in complete fullness.
- Peace will dominate the city.
- There will be no exploitation, slavery.
- There will be no war.
- There will be no sickness.
- The sins of the citizens will all be forgiven.

Why?

> For the LORD is our judge,
> the LORD is our lawgiver,
> the LORD is our King;
> it is He who will make us whole. (Isaiah 33:22)

At this time, we who believe will be caught up, enthralled by Him! Our love for Him will be overpowering! We will all love the kingdom of heaven more than the kingdoms of this world! What a glorious hope! The kingdoms of this world will be all consumed by the kingdom of heaven (Revelation 11:15). The Lord Himself will secure the victory. We will all have access to the tree of life, which will be the source of the healing of the nations. The throne of God and of the Lamb will be in the city and His servants will serve Him (Revelation 22:1-5). The kingdom of heaven will be fully restored on earth, and we will forever be with the King (1 Thessalonians 4:16-18)!

Meanwhile, in varying degrees and in various ways, we can enjoy a foretaste of this glorious kingdom to come. It starts with our relationship with the Sovereign King, and it continues by us living the kingdom out in word and deed in the world in which we live.

REFLECTIONS

Discuss the connection between political stability and freedom and the character of the people. Think about:

In which countries has there been an enduring political freedom?

What underlying ideas and accompanying values do these nations have in common?

What has caused disruptions to the stability of governments of 'free' nations?

Investigate the political history of a nation such as Haiti.

What are the needs of the people who live in politically unstable nations?

What is their greatest need?

What do you think will bring about political stability?

What can you and I do about the plight of people in places experiencing war and political instability?

Consider how to live in a social/political environment that is an antithesis to the kingdom of God. Read Colossians 3:1-17. What might you do to help those who live in such places today?

11

BELIEVERS AND THE PUBLIC SQUARE

How then should we live in relation to the state?

There is a wide range of approaches to how Christians should be involved with the state. Some advocate complete separation from the state, even to the extent that Christians should not even vote. Alternatively, there are those who suggest it is essential that every Christian must contribute towards Christian control of the state!

Government operates in the social structures related to the issues facing society, such as systemic injustice. Earlier sections in this book argue that the root cause of systemic evil is in the hearts of humans who exploit opportunities to promote their own agenda or gratification, consciously or inadvertently at the expense of others. This exploitation becomes entrenched in social structures which become social norms. Such problems of social injustice need to be confronted at all levels:

- the self-serving sin of people,

- the systemic injustice, and
- meeting the needs of the victims of the injustice.

God calls some of His people to focus on the systemic aspect of social issues, to be involved in some way in government. The story of William Wilberforce is a well-known historical example of this. He addressed the prevalent self-gratification and evil behaviour in all strata of British society. He worked hard to get the king and parliament to do something to stem this unrighteousness. Concurrently, he was aware of the problem of slavery which needed to be addressed at the three levels listed above. He knew that God had called him to focus on the legislative aspect of the injustice of slavery.

It is pertinent to observe how Jesus navigated his teaching and activities in the political context in which he lived. Along with relevant teaching found throughout the New Testament, Christ's life should give us guidance as to how Christians should relate to civil government.

Jesus' example of relating to agents of the state

Jesus came into this world, into Israel, at a time when there were layers of political authorities operating in the land. There was the Roman Empire. Rome, at this time, was ruled by an emperor, whose title was Caesar. The emperor was the ultimate political authority. However, Rome allowed a degree of local government. The original Herod, Herod the Great, who was an Idumean, had negotiated a degree of secular rule over the Jewish people. After his time, Herod's kingdom became fragmented. Rome saw fit to assign rulers over local areas. Judea proved particularly difficult to govern because many Jews religiously resented external authority. Groups such as the Zealots would aggressively resist the Romans. Consequently, Rome had to impose direct control over Judea in the form of a proconsul. At the time of Jesus' ministry, Pontius Pilate was the proconsul.

There was also the religious leadership in Judea. The Sanhedrin was a body of about 70 men who exercised authority over the religious activities of the Jews, centred around the temple in Jerusalem. The Roman authorities limited their powers. The chief priest was approved by Rome and may have even been appointed by them.

Jesus was seen as a threat to these Jewish political rulers. Herod the Great saw the potential King of the Jews being developed as a real political threat, and so organised the execution of male babies in the region around Bethlehem. The religious leaders resented Jesus' popularity. They saw His influence as a political threat and attempted to limit His influence on several occasions. It was these religious leaders who instigated His trial, suffering and crucifixion. Unable to officially execute Him, they managed to get the Roman authorities to crucify Him.

Underpinning Jesus' attitude and actions in relation to those who opposed Him was the foundational principle of relating to others, with love:

You have heard that it was said, 'Love your neighbour and hate your enemy'. But I tell you, love your enemies and pray for those who persecute you. (Matthew 5:43-44)

Jesus practised what He preached. He loved both the oppressed and the oppressor.

For example, He would relate to tax collectors. Tax collectors were men who had won a contract with the government to extract tax money from the people. They were collaborators with the Roman government. They had a reputation of using their government backing to extort extra money from people to line their own pockets. They were hated and ostracised from the community. But Jesus was known as a friend of tax collectors (Matthew 11:19). He even called a tax collector, Matthew, to be in His inner circle of disciples (Matthew 9:9). Though He chose to relate to them, He did not condone their sin. His love and acceptance led to conviction of sin, as with Zacchaeus the tax collector, who chose to repay fourfold those whom he had cheated out of money. Jesus dramatically confronted the practice of extorting money from people in the name of God when He turned over money tables in the temple grounds and drove the animals out of the yard (Matthew 21:13, Luke 19:46).

When God saw us all in our plight because of sin, He did not remain in heaven and just throw money at us. Rather, He came and lived among us.

> The Word became flesh and made His dwelling among us. We have seen His glory, the glory of the one and only Son, who came from the Father, full of grace and truth. (John 1:14)

He addressed both our physical need and spiritual plight by communication of the truth and practical action. In this way, He set an example for us to follow.

There is no record of Jesus speaking against, or even criticising, the Roman rulers. He spoke forthrightly against his fellow rabbis, scribes and Pharisees, who claimed to be agents of God yet lived contrary to the intent of the law of God. When He overturned the money changers' tables in the temple He was objecting to their misrepresentation of God. Social injustice in the name of God is reprehensible. He called out their pride and hypocritical judgementalism. This is consistent with the teaching of Paul about judgmentalism in Romans 2, noted in an earlier chapter.

Jesus paid taxes as required. Matthew, Mark and Luke recorded that Pharisees and Herodians tried to trap Jesus in His words by questioning Him about paying the imperial tax imposed on non-Roman citizens. As was His practice on many occasions when faced with a hostile question, He did not give them a straight answer, but rather He asked them a question and responded to their answer. Pointing to the Roman inscription on a coin, He said:

> So, give back to Caesar the things that are Caesar's, and to God what is God's. (Matthew 22:21)

He left them with nothing that they could use against Him, and if they really wanted to know His stand on the matter, they could work it out themselves. Most commentators agree that Jesus was implying that we should obey all civil authorities and play our part in the public square, as we are called and are able, while at the same time our spiritual worship, our purpose for living and way of life should be for God.

The final and most significant action in relation to the political powers of His time was Jesus' pursuit of the kingdom of God to the cross. While the political powers thought they were conquering Him, He was achieving a far more significant victory. By His sacrifice He conquered the powers behind the idolatrous kingdoms of this world. In doing so, He set us free from the power of the demonic rulers of this world. He set us an example of the methodology of His Kingdom, sacrificial love and the resurrecting power of the Holy Spirit.

Further biblical teaching

The Bible has clear teaching about God's people living in a kingdom of this world.

> "I know the plans I have for you", declares the LORD, "plans to prosper you and not to harm you, plans to give you hope and a future." (Jeremiah 29:11)

This verse is often quoted with good effect, but often out of context. Jeremiah was conveying the word of the LORD to Israelites who found themselves in exile in Babylon. God was telling them how to live under the rule of a foreign and even hostile regime.

Here is a summary of His instructions, given in chapter 29:

- Contribute to the economy, with housing construction and food production.
- Contribute to the population, with children and grandchildren.
- Contribute to the peace and prosperity of the city, the common good.
- Pray for the city.
- Don't listen to prophets who tell you otherwise.
- The city's time of dominion is limited, so live with the hope of a great future, as I have my plans for you...

While anticipating a city still to come they were to live for the good of the city in which they found themselves living. It seems clear that Daniel, who knew the prophecies of Jeremiah well, was committed to embracing this advice. The book of Daniel relates how he made a positive contribution to the Babylonian and subsequent Persian empires in public office without compromising His commitment to the LORD. In fact, working out his commitment to God enabled him to make that positive difference.

As believers, we find ourselves with 'dual citizenship'. In the present life, we do not have an enduring city, but we are looking for the city that is to come (see Hebrews 13:14 and also Philippians 3:20-21).

Jeremiah's words to the exiles in Babylon have great similarities to the instructions given in the New Testament epistles to a people who found themselves citizens of the heavenly kingdom while still living in this temporary world system.

These instructions are found in Romans 13:1-7, 1 Timothy 2:1-4, Titus 3:1-2, and 1 Peter 2:11-25. Here is a list of points made in these passages.

- Be subject to governing authorities.
- God has established these governments.
- Their role is to punish the wrongdoer and commend the doer of good.
- Pay taxes so they can do their work.
- Pray for rulers that all may live in peace, quietly doing what is godly and holy. This contributes to all people having the opportunity to come to a knowledge of the truth.
- Be ready to do whatever is good.
- Slander no one, be peaceable, considerate, and gentle toward everyone.
- Live so people see your good works and in due time glorify God.
- Doing God's will can rebut ignorant accusative talk.
- Show respect to everyone, love the family of believers, fear God, and honour the emperor.
- Put trust in the ultimate judgment of God.

Salt and light in the 'public square'

Right in the Sermon on the Mount, Jesus stated basic principles about our relationship to 'the world', society beyond our personal family and the family of God – our involvement in 'the public square'.

You are the salt of the earth. But if the salt loses its saltiness, how can it be made salty again? It is no longer good for anything, except to be thrown out and trampled underfoot.

You are the light of the world. A town built on a hill cannot be hidden. Neither do people light a lamp and put it under a bowl. Instead, they put it on its stand, and it gives light to everyone in the house. In the same way, let your light shine before others, that may see your good deeds and glorify your Father in heaven. (Matthew 5:13-16)

This is a clear statement of how we who are the children of the kingdom should involve ourselves with the world. It has direct application to our involvement in the public square.

As salt we contribute towards the 'taste' (the positive experience) and the preservation of our society. To do this we must, like salt, get mixed in with the fabric of our society. Yes – get in there and be involved. But there is a danger. If we absorb the dirt of the world we lose our value, our effectiveness. Acquiescing to the thought patterns and values of the world, destroys our ability to make a difference. We must resolutely stand firm and be different where it counts – with God's difference. And that's where being light comes in. As light we enable people to see the truth and the way to go. We do this by standing out and being different in our ideas, values and way of life. This is our prophetic voice. By deed and by word we speak to the people observing us, including the leaders of this world. But there is a wrong way of shining our light. If we choose to live a life so much separate from the world that we are not seen, the world will only believe the negative stereotypes of Christians that the media may promote. And so, we become totally ineffective in influencing the world. We must resolutely get involved with the world – in the world but not of the world. We need to be both salt and light!

Early Christians and civil government

The New Testament was written at a time when it was highly unlikely that Christians would get involved in the affairs of government which was tightly controlled by the Roman authorities. However, there were people already involved in the administration of the Roman government who heard the gospel and chose to believe in Christ. There was Levi, a tax collector who became Matthew, a disciple of Jesus. There was Cornelius, a Roman centurion in Caesarea, who was a Godfearer who along with his household heard the gospel and received the gift of the Holy Spirit while Peter was relating the story of Christ to them. In the last greetings in the epistle to the Romans, Paul mentions Erastus, who was a city's director of public works. Presumably, these men had little immediate influence on the major political decisions being made in Rome and its outposts. But they certainly had opportunity to tell the story of Christ, albeit with potential risks, and had opportunity to outwork the gospel in exemplary public service.

The equivalents of our law courts were ruled by agents of the empire or local authorities approved by Rome. Pontius Pilate as procurator was an agent of Caesar in Judea. His priorities were to maintain 'Pax Romana', the law and order that came through the power and authority of Rome. Some other territories had arbitrators accountable to more local authorities. In any case, they weren't guided by the law of God. Their morality and loyalties were not necessarily trustworthy. That is one reason why Paul advised the Corinthian Christians to sort out their differences 'in house'. The decisions of the arbitrators of the worldly kingdom would likely be driven by selfish desires or reputation-saving, not by righteousness (see 1 Corinthians 6:1-11).

In the 200 years following New Testament times, many Christians were highly successful in fulfilling their calling in relation to the political powers of their world. They were seen showing practical love and telling the story of Christ to explain their way of living. Their attitudes and actions would be in stark contrast to the people who had political power. Consequently, they were ignored or were despised and at times coerced to reject their faith or be punished for not idolising the powers that be. In remaining faithful, they were 'overcomers' as the book of Revelation described them. Success in the kingdom of God is not gaining social or political power. It is demonstrating the power of Christ's love!

How we can be involved

In much of the modern world Christians live in political contexts somewhat similar to the ancient world. The community leadership does not hold itself accountable to either God or the people. Citizens are merely 'subjects' whose role is not to question but comply. They may have opportunity to serve in the regime or they may be compelled to do so, such as serving in the military. But they can follow the instructions given by Peter to live so that people can see their good works (1 Peter 2:12). They can be peaceable, considerate, gentle toward everyone and pray for their rulers. They can trust God to use their witness so that some may in due time respond to Him.

In the 'free world' we have opportunity to do much more. Our 'democracies' give citizens an opportunity to:

- have a say in who forms the legislature, by voting,
- freely speak in public about the issues facing governments,
- have influence through 'lobbying' and advising the decision makers,
- be personally involved in politics, and
- be an influencer or educator about public affairs.

By voting

As believers we can approach voting with a different attitude to that typically found in the world. We will not be asking ourselves the question, "What's in it for me?", but rather, "What will be best for the flourishing of the people or for the common good of the city or the nation?" We can use our vote to support those who, it appears, are informed by the Word of God. We can use our vote to support those who display a degree of righteousness. That righteousness may be expressed in policies they advocate and vote for in the legislature, and it may be seen by the integrity with which they carry out their responsibilities. Sadly, many do not investigate these matters and merely vote on party partisan lines and thus can contribute to giving power to politicians without a godly moral compass. We need to be discerning using biblically based criteria of judgement.

By speaking out for change

God calls some people to do more than just vote. The church, the body of the followers of Christ, is called to have a 'prophetic voice', communicating what God has to say on the issue. In our 'free world' that can include political activism. Political activism that rationally and respectfully confronts ideas contrary to the knowledge of God is an effective way to outwork the kingdom of God in this world. When done astutely, it honours God as King.

Many historical 'heroes of the faith' in the Western world were political activists. Not the least of these were the 19th-century Christian reformers in Britain. Names such as William Wilberforce, Elizabeth Fry, Florence Nightingale, and Ashley Cooper (Lord Shaftesbury) are well known and respected by many because, as believers, they seriously outworked their faith advocating for others such as slaves, prisoners, sick and wounded, women, Jews and the exploited. They backed up their political persuasion with practical action.

Christian political activism needs to be based on *truth* and expressed with *grace*.

Firstly, those who choose to be politically active need to ensure they are grounded in the truth, asking themselves questions such as these:

- Is the 'truth' we are reacting to or declaring really derived from actual observation and reason? Sometimes we can be stirred by information that has developed in, for example, some online echo-chamber.
- Are we moved by God's truth or merely human outrage?
- Are we moved by anxiety about what is happening? Do we fear the uncertain future, or are we trusting in the faithfulness of God?

They do well to check that they have identified the real enemy, the root cause of the problem faced. Jesus knew that his ultimate enemies were not the people who were politically hostile to Him but the spiritual powers behind them. As Paul wrote to the Ephesians:

> Our struggle is not against flesh and blood, but against the rulers, against the authorities, against the powers of this dark world and against the spiritual forces of evil in the heavenly realms. (Ephesians 6:12)

This seems to suggest that conspiracies, such as 'the deep state' of which some people are prone to speak, are built up not by people but spiritual beings opposed to God. For example, it was revealed to Daniel that, behind the scenes, the prince of the kingdom of Persia was resisting the work of the angel, Michael (see Daniel chapter 10).

Such spiritual powers operate in the realm of captivating ideas which are opposed to God.

> For though we live in the world, we do not wage war as the world does. The weapons we fight with are not the weapons of the world. On the contrary, they have divine power to demolish strongholds. (2 Corinthians 10:4-5)

Rather than attack the persons, wise Christian activists address the ideas that have captivated people's minds. They can demolish the arguments that resist the knowledge of God, while showing loving respect toward the persons held captive by them. Their weapons include prayer, the truth of God's Word, faith and righteous attitude and action (see Ephesians 6:13-18). They address the act of disobedience, not the person, and then only when they have confronted and dealt with their own disobedience (2 Corinthians 10:5-6). They let the Spirit bring about change. This is the methodology of the kingdom of heaven.

Rather than putting down the people who oppose God with their ideas and practices, wise lobbying will positively present a better way, a way that they know is God's way. We sometimes call it constructive criticism. Their involvement in the public square is not just reactive, but 'prophetic', proactively proclaiming and outworking the mission of the kingdom of God.

Secondly, Christian activism needs to be practised with grace. Activists need to ask themselves, are we acting in a way so that the world can see the grace of God rather than outrage and judgmentalism? Effective communication considers the needs and motivations of the hearers. It needs to be in the language and idiom of the people who are hearing us. Yes, they may read actions and words according to their preconceived ideas, but wise action does not give them evidence that confirms their negative ideas. Remember, Jesus did not give His hostile audience words that could be taken out of context and used to misrepresent Him. To the best of their ability, activists need to speak and act so that the hearers can see them reflecting the love of God.

They need to act with both truth and grace. Truth without grace can be read as judgmentalism. Grace without truth can be read as permissiveness.

Effective Christian political action is grounded in truth, motivated by love, and expressed with grace. It seeks justice. It takes courage and humility.

By being involved in politics

I have heard it said by some Christians involved in politics that there is no such thing as a Christian nation, a Christian government or even a Christian political party. There are only Christian people. The kingdom of God is not expressed as a political structure. If it were, it would be a kingdom of this world. I don't plan to argue the point about this but rather suggest that the role of Christianity is to infiltrate and influence earthly political structures. God calls some of us to be actively involved in politics. This may be as individuals or as a party. Jesus said we, His followers, are salt and light. Salt gets into the food and gives it preservation and taste. Some are called to be in the existing political parties. Light stands out in the open and shows the world what is right. That may involve being a separate party or an independent thinker in a party. Whichever way, people can see the difference and be inspired to be like that.

Amongst other things, a party member can be involved in:

- shaping or articulating party values and priorities,
- shaping party (and potential government) policy and practice,
- choosing persons to represent the people in the legislative body, and
- advising those who are elected to office.

As a Christian believer one needs to be guided by an accurate understanding of the biblically-defined nature and role of government. This book endeavours to be a mere introduction to this. One also needs to understand the context in which these principles are to be applied. This context includes the culture of the society at large, legal constraints, and the constitutional structures of the governing body in which they are to work.

When considering the policies and practices of a government or potential government, it seems good to keep in mind the core role of governing authorities as per the New Testament teaching – the commending of doing good and the punishment of evil-doing. When considering a proposed government measure, one can ask the questions, "What behaviour does this policy overtly or unintentionally reward?" and "What does it overtly or unintentionally punish?" One could ask the question, "Is this an issue where the government should command and control, or rather inspire and enable?" And we could ask, "Is there a better way that the government and the community can address this issue?"

Christian involvement in political policy making should never be an outworking of religious judgmentalism. Sadly, Christian history is littered with examples of this. The worst manifestations of this include banning, imprisonment and even execution of heretics, literal witch hunts, and the banning of and wars against 'pagans'. It is not our role to be involved in a 'Christian' version of 'cancel culture'.

On the other hand, it is a wonderful privilege to explore what biblical principles would look like as policies in the contemporary context. (See the next chapter for an example of eliciting what the Bible says about an issue.) Then comes the challenge of practically enacting these principles in a way that promotes the common good, and which enables the promotion and outworking of the kingdom of God.

It appears that sometimes the enactment of laws that are contrary to the will of most of the people can be counterproductive. This can apply to well-meaning laws that align with Christian teaching. In the USA, despite the banning of abortion in several states, and Christians rejoicing about this, the number of abortions in the USA is continuing to rise. People who don't see the logic or justice of these laws appear to be determined to find a way to do what they want to do. As stated previously, legislation does not bring about righteousness and the state is not the agent of salvation. There needs to be a change of heart in the people for righteousness to prevail.

The kingdom of God cannot be achieved by political means, but the principles of the kingdom of heaven, together with the work of the Holy Spirit, can guide the citizen of the kingdom working in an earthly kingdom. It is not the role of a Christian politician to impose his personal moral standards on others, but rather to listen to those to whom he is accountable, and if necessary, graciously persuade them of a better way. We cannot achieve justice by making laws that enforce others to do justice. Remember, God has achieved justice, and we who are declared to be righteous can live justly. The role of a 'just' government is to enable those who are righteous to freely do justly.

The story is told of a recent occasion in Britain when a party won the election and found themselves as the government. In the party room they were celebrating and chanting, "We have the power!" The newly elected Prime Minister (who happened to be a Christian believer) effectively reprimanded them by telling them that we are not here to exercise power over the people. The nation was constituted so that the people had the power. We are here to serve the nation, to facilitate the common good, the flourishing of the people. I don't know how accurate the story is, but it illustrates the point that, those who are called to active service in politics need to ask themselves at least these questions:

- What is my motivation and purpose?
- What is my accountability? To whom am I accountable?

Purpose
Christian political leaders need to ask themselves these questions:

- What motivates or drives my political service?
- What is my passion, or deep desire?
- Is it power and prestige, or is it serving God to achieve the common good of the people?
- Is it to fulfil my need to lead or is it to see righteous outcomes in the community and nation?
- Is it to build my kingdom or to enable the kingdom of God to flourish in the community?

Several decades ago, a premier of one of the states of Australia was interviewed on television about the influence of his Christian faith. He emphatically made the point that his motivation and mode of operation was to serve the people of the state. Viewers were impressed. Sadly, as the years went by his leadership style changed and, amongst other things, he 'rigged' the electoral system to maintain power, and consequently went down in history as one who illustrated the saying that the lust for power corrupts. The change of attitude and practice was incremental. We all need to constantly remind ourselves of our sinful human inclination to corruption.

An attitude of service should be the foundational mode of the Christian leader. Since the day of the fall, Adam and his descendants have struggled with the abuse of power in leadership. As noted previously, the typical political leadership of the kingdoms of the world are authoritarian. In the 'free world', authoritarian rule is usually frowned upon, yet the trend of governments often seems to be to move toward greater power, more regulations and the centralisation of that power. It takes a wise and confident leader to check this trend. We need to remind ourselves that we are called to serve God by serving people.

Accountability

Christian politicians need to know to whom they are accountable, and to seek accountability. There is a great sense of security when one seeks to be under the authority of a greater power. Politicians need to regularly remind themselves of their accountability.

As Christians, we see our primary accountability is to God. If God has called us to serve Him in a governance space, we have a responsibility to be faithful to that call. That call is ongoing. We need to position ourselves to continue to hear that call. A wise Christian leader is a person of prayer. Keeping in touch with God is a foundational way of hearing his voice and following the leadership of the Holy Spirit. Asking the question, "How would You have me stand and act on this issue?" should be standard procedure. God will in due time reward us for our faithfulness.

In a modern 'democracy', political leaders are accountable to the people who nominated them and to the people who voted them into their position. As a representative of the people, the politician effectively has a contract with them, to serve for the common good. A minister or officer cannot use their position to help or favour one person or group. In our free 'democratic' world that kind of behaviour is rightly considered corruption. At times, politicians have found themselves in a law court for using their position to help a friend. Sadly, this type of corruption is rife and unchecked in countries where there has not been a long history of Christian values. There are many stories of elected political leaders promoting their mates and silencing and even eliminating their opponents. Corruption can be the greatest impediment to social justice. It is a fundamental biblical principle that all people are created in the image of God and are equally valuable to Him and are to be served by officers of the state without prejudice or special favour. Unbridled corruption has been the downfall of many a government.

> By justice a king gives a country stability,
> But those who are greedy for bribes tear it down.
> (Proverbs 29:4)

> Remove the dross from the silver,
> And a silversmith can produce a vessel;
> Remove wicked officials from the king's presence,
> And his throne will be established through righteousness. (Proverbs 25:4-5)

A politician can choose a political party because they agree with the values and principles it espouses. Consequently, they are contracted to uphold these and consider them when choosing a particular course of action. They also have the challenging responsibility to hold fellow party members accountable to the principles. Doing this in an encouraging way is a vital part of teamwork.

Thus, they have ongoing accountability to God, to the party and to the people. The challenge comes when they believe these loyalties clash. Then they must ask themselves, what is our prior commitment, and how do we honestly communicate to others where we stand. The biblical stories of Daniel and his fellow faithful friends are great examples to inspire us. Our integrity may temporarily get us into difficulty, but in the long run it will cause us to be respected and be effective ambassadors of Christ.

I recommend reading the book, *Every Square Inch* by Bruce Riley Ashford. (See the recommended reading at the end of the book.) In the chapter on politics and the public square he summarises a Christian involvement with these seven points:

- We want to avoid a coercive relationship between the church and state.
- We should be active in promoting the common good.
- We should be discerning in how we articulate our beliefs.
- We should be discerning in what we say from our pulpits.
- We should be civil in our demeanour.
- We should be realistic in what we expect from the political sphere.
- We should remember that politics is only one dimension of our cultural witness.

He reminds us to do it all with grace and joy.

We all can be influencers

All believers are called to do their part, as a parent, an employer or employee, a mentor or teacher, or in whatever social setting or role you are led to serve. We all can in some way promote wisdom and virtue by modelling it and teaching about it. We can mentor our children and other people in wise decision-making. We can ensure our children are educated in, not only science and technology to become mere consumers and pleasure seekers, but the wisdom and virtue that come from God so that they can live such virtue in all of life. We can introduce people to the source of wisdom and virtue, Jesus Christ. We can set an example by practically living out the kingdom of God in all aspects of our everyday lives.

What has God called you to do?

- Ask Him to lead you.
- Understand His mission in the world.
- Examine yourself as to what you are best suited to do.
- Be moved by the love of God and do it.

REFLECTIONS

Considering political support:

When considering the political leaders you wish to support, do you consider their character?

How do they relate to others?

Is there an inclination to control everyone, or are their actions characterised by service?

In this aspect, are they of the nature of Adam, Cain and Nimrod?

Do they recognise the higher authority of God?

Considering the action of fellow Christians:

Consider a recent event (or events) in the news where Christians have been involved with social or political action. Has it been reported by the media in a supportive or antagonistic way?

When you hear in the news of some Christians aggressively opposing practices in the community that are contrary to biblical teaching, what things give you reason to celebrate? What things, if any, about it cause you to cringe?

From what you can tell was there an expression of both truth and grace? From what you can tell, was it an expression of outrage and/or love?

Has it been effective in causing people to change their attitude or behaviour?

Has the name of Christ been brought into good or bad repute?

Considering my action:

In the light of Romans 12:3ff and the spheres of service mentioned in this chapter, examine yourself and ask God what He would have you do. Share with the group where you are at with this process.

What are your motivations and what do you plan to do?

Have you asked someone to be your mentor, to hold you accountable to your commitment?

Considering support of the church:

Does your church regularly celebrate and encourage the involvement of members in the public square?

How could this be done as part of its regular programme?

12

ADDRESSING THE ISSUES FROM A BIBLICAL PERSPECTIVE

Governments face a multitude of issues affecting almost all areas of our lives. These areas of life include:

- Law and order.
- Criminal law.
- Social justice.
- National defence.
- International affairs.
- Immigration.
- Education.
- Poverty and welfare.
- Family life and law.
- Indigenous people's affairs.
- Property rights.
- Business practice.
- Work and rest – including employment and holidays.

This is just a sample of significant issues that governments address. These areas are not isolated issues but are interwoven in the web of social life. Governments attempt to departmentalise their administration of their roles in these areas.

What is the biblical way to approach an issue about which governments make policies and enact practices? It is not the purpose of this book to outline principles related to all these issues, but rather point to some general principles of discerning what the Bible has to say. I have chosen to illustrate this using the example of poverty and welfare. My analysis is not comprehensive. There is heaps more that could be outlined. This example is just an introduction to the topic.

Clearly, a few verses selected to prove what you want to say is an arrogant way to approach the Bible. It is not submissive to the Word and can be the source of error. Rather, we endeavour to appreciate the whole gist of the Word of God on a matter. Here is a framework that I use to find out what the Bible has to say about an issue. At each step I am asking God to speak to me and give me more wisdom and to nudge me to obey His word to me.

- What was God's intention in the beginning – before the fall?
- What difference did the fall make?
- What purposes and principles lie behind the measures of the law of Moses?
- What did the prophets say about the issue?
- What difference did the work of Jesus make?
- What practical guidance can we get from the teaching of Jesus, the practical teaching of the

New Testament epistles and wisdom books such as Proverbs?
- How does this all apply in our contemporary context?

This is the sort of approach taken in this book to discover a biblical approach to government.

So, what does the Bible teach us about poverty and welfare?

What was God's intention in the beginning – before the fall – and what difference did the fall make?

The beginning of Genesis describes how God provided the abundance of the Garden of Eden. God was truly our provider. Poverty was not an issue, provided we did our part of tending the plants, understanding and caring for the environment, following the daily guidance of our Creator. The intention was that, as the human family increased, we would have plenty to provide for the family. The family would be taught to walk in the garden with God, listen to His instructions, and continue the work of managing the world in which He had placed us. The abundance of the garden would expand as humans populated the whole earth. The key to prosperity was listening to and following the word of the Lord.

But they chose to 'do it my way'! The consequence of failing to listen to the word of the Lord was to be separated from His presence. They found themselves out of Eden. They found themselves out of the ecosystem of abundance. Broken relationship with God led to brokenness in the supply chain of abundance. They found themselves on their own, trying to 'make ends meet'.

This broken relationship with God had the 'domino effect' of broken relationships with each other. The man blamed the woman for the problem. One son resented the other's efforts to re-connect with God by sacrificing some of his provisions. Further family splits lead to different branches of the family competing with each other for resources.

Broken relationship with God and with each other and the selfish desire to have are clearly the root causes of poverty and the gap between the rich and the poor.

What does the law of Moses contribute to our understanding of the topic?

The law of Moses stands out from other regimes in its day. It clearly insists on caring for the needy. Many of the instructions in the law relate to the issue. Providing for the needy comes with a promise of blessing.

> Give generously to [the needy] and do so without a grudging heart; then because of this the LORD your God will bless you in all your work and in everything you put your hand to. There will always be poor in the land. Therefore, I command you to be openhanded toward your fellow Israelites who are poor and needy in your land. (Deuteronomy 15:10-11)
>
> Instructions on how to be generous to the poor led the peo-

ple to give opportunity for the needy to improve themselves by working with dignity. The practice of allowing the needy to glean in the orchards and fields is a clear example.

> When you reap the harvest of your land, do not reap to the very edges of your field or gather the gleanings of your harvest. Do not go over your vineyard a second time or pick up the grapes that have fallen. Leave them for the poor and the foreigner. (Leviticus 19:9-10 and 23:22)

This brilliant practice not only ensured the needy had food but did it in a way that gave them the dignity of doing some work for their living. Caring for the poor was not the responsibility of the 'professional' community leaders, the priests and Levites, but rather the responsibility of every family enterprise in the community.

Part of the purpose of the sabbatical days and years was to care for the poor and underprivileged.

> For six years you are to sow your fields and harvest the crops, but during the seventh year let the land lie unplowed and unused. Then the poor among your people may get food from it, and the wild animals may eat what is left. Do the same with your vineyard and your olive grove. (Exodus 23:12)

Underlying the regulations about the adoption of orphans and marriage of widows by the nearest family was ensuring no one of the poor was left to their own devices to survive. Extended family were there to care for them.

They were instructed not to charge interest when lending to the poor, and on the seventh year cancel unpaid debts so that there was no need for any Israelite living in the land to be chronically in need.

The poor working for the landowner were to be paid a proper wage, and not exploited or made to work excessive hours.

> Do not take advantage of a hired worker who is poor and needy, whether that worker is a fellow Israelite or a foreigner residing in one of your towns. Pay them wages each day before sunset, because they are poor and are counting on it... (Deuteronomy 24:14-15)

> Six days do your work, but on the seventh day do not work, so that your ox and your donkey may rest, and so that the servant in your household and the foreigner living among you may be refreshed. (Exodus 23:12)

These laws reflect the heart of God toward the poor and vulnerable, and they were in stark contrast to the norm in the ancient world. He loves us all equally, created in His image, designed equally to reflect His holiness and glory. As Hannah said in her prayer:

> He raises the poor from the dust and lifts the needy from the ash heap; he sets them with princes and has them inherit a throne of honour. (1 Samuel 2:8)

As previously mentioned, the purpose behind all of God's instructions to Israel was to challenge them to be an example of God's will for all nations. God's heart is to give all an equal opportunity to develop and express His glory in their lives. And He wants us not to frustrate this purpose by keeping the poor low.

What did the prophets say about the topic?

The wisdom literature and the prophets in the Old Testament reinforce the intent of the law.
God cares for the needy. The Psalm that says:

> The LORD is exalted over all the nations,
> His glory above the heavens.
> Who is like the LORD our God,
> the One who sits enthroned on high,

goes on to say:

> He raises the poor from the dust
> and lifts the needy from the ash heap,
> He seats them with princes,
> with the princes of his people. (Psalm 113:4-8)

> Who is like you, LORD?
> You rescue the poor from those too strong for them,
> The poor and needy from those who rob them.
> (Psalm 35:10)

For Him caring about the poor is a matter of justice, of righteousness!

> The righteous care about justice for the poor,
> but the wicked have no such concern. (Proverbs 29:7)

> Speak up for those who cannot speak for themselves,
> for the rights of all who are destitute.
> Speak up and judge fairly;
> Defend the rights of the poor and needy.
> (Proverbs 31:8-9)

The prophets repeatedly condemned the exploitation of the poor. They particularly confront those in positions of power.

Right from the first prophecy recorded in Isaiah, he addresses this issue:

> Wash and make yourselves clean.
> Take your evil deeds out of my sight; stop doing wrong.
> Learn to do right; seek justice.
> Defend the oppressed.
> Take up the cause of the fatherless;
> plead the case of the widow. (Isaiah 1:16-17)

> You rulers are rebels, partners with thieves…
> They do not defend the cause of the fatherless;
> the widow's case does not come before them.
> (Isaiah 1:23)

> The LORD enters into judgment against the elders and leaders of His people:
> "It is you who have ruined my vineyard;
> The plunder from the poor is in your houses.
> What do you mean by crushing my people and grinding the faces of the poor?" (Isaiah 3:14-15)

> This is what the LORD says:
> For three sins of Israel, even four I will not relent.
> They sell the innocent for silver, and the needy
> for a pair of sandals.
> They trample on the heads of the poor as on
> the dust of the ground
> and deny justice to the oppressed... (Amos 2:6-7)

These are just two examples from the prophets. It is a repeated theme of the latter prophets. We all, civil leaders and the citizens, need to make God's concern for the poor our concern too.

What difference did the teaching and work of Jesus make?

Jesus is the epicentre of God's plan for the poor. God did not remain in heaven and send people with resources to meet the need of the poverty-stricken human race. He sacrificially came himself.

> [Jesus] being in the very nature God, did not consider equality with God something to be used to his own

advantage; rather he made himself nothing by taking the very nature of a servant... (Philippians 2:6-7)

He was born to a relatively poor family who during his infancy were refugees. He came proclaiming good news to the poor. Right at the beginning of his ministry He declared that social justice was at the heart of His calling. He came to deal with the source of poverty, bondage, sickness and oppression.

The Spirit of the LORD is on me,
Because He has anointed me to proclaim
good news to the poor.
He has sent me to proclaim freedom for the prisoners
and recovery of sight to the blind,
to set the oppressed free. (Luke 4:18)

He chose to relate to the poor, to meet the needs of the poor and urged people such as the rich young nobleman to do the same (Mark 10:22 and Luke 18:22). When Jesus said: "You will always have the poor with you" (e.g. Matthew 26:11), He was not giving us an excuse to ignore the poor, but rather He was reminding his disciples that He and his disciples were constantly relating to and helping the poor.

He taught that prosperity and poverty run deep – deeper than and beyond the supply or lack of money. When confronted by a man with a family inheritance issue, He said, "... life does not consist in the abundance of possessions." He then told the story of a man who stored up possessions only to be faced with impending death.

"This is how it will be with whoever stores up things for themselves but is not rich toward God." (Luke 12:13-21)

Jesus spoke of the challenge of being rich. The conversation he had with the rich young ruling class man, who was not prepared to give up what he had, concludes with Jesus saying it is easier for a camel to go through the eye of a needle than for the rich to enter the kingdom. See, for example, Matthew 19:16-26. The problem facing both the rich and the poor is a selfish desire to have something that they think the market, the government or someone else can offer them.

Poverty and prosperity are deeply connected to our relationship with God. The first of the beatitudes he taught was "Blessed are the poor in spirit, for theirs is the kingdom of heaven." Recognising our desperate need to relate to the king of heaven is the first step toward being in His kingdom. Lasting prosperity begins with a restored relationship with God. And that was the central purpose of Jesus' life, death and resurrection – to restore the prosperity of our spirit. From this foundation, flourishing can blossom in all of life.

What practical guidance can we get from the practical teaching of the New Testament epistles?

Caring for the poor was a high priority of the first church. The first deacons were appointed to supervise the distribution of resources to the needy in the church in Jerusalem (See Acts 4:32 and 6:1-7). In summarising the outcome of the first church council in Jerusalem, Paul concludes with:

All they asked was that we should continue to remember the poor, the very thing I had been eager to do all along. (Galatians 2:10)

James challenges us to examine our attitude and actions toward the lowly.

Religion that God our Father accepts as pure and faultless is this: to look after orphans and widows in their distress and to keep oneself from being polluted by the world. (James 1:17)

He then goes on to advise them not to give preference to the rich over the poor, but to show love with the appropriate deeds. See James chapter 2.

In the epistles to the Thessalonian church and to Timothy, Paul outlines priorities guiding practical strategies to counter poverty.

The first priority is self-help. He warns the church to be wary of those who blatantly choose to sponge off their charity rather than earn their own living. He refers to some in the church as 'idle and disruptive' (see 2 Thessalonians 3:6-15). He urges commendation of those who choose to work hard, especially those who work hard to build up others (1 Thessalonians 5:12-15).

The second 'port of call' is family – immediate and extended. Families are designed by God to help one another, practically and spiritually. Paul makes this very clear when giving instructions about widows (see 1 Timothy 5:3-8).

The third source of help is the local community, the church. Paul urges the church leadership (Timothy in this case) to "give proper recognition to those widows who are really in need" (1 Timothy 5:3). The real needy whom the church should help were those who lack family to mutually care for one another.

The Bible makes it clear what is the root cause of poverty. The problem is not simply economic. Its source is spiritual and ethical. The chief factor behind economic poverty is relational poverty. Poverty all begins with the breakdown in our relationship with God. Correcting this is the beginning of the solution. As we have observed, in the Bible the poor are usually referred to as widows, orphans and foreigners. Widows and orphans are disconnected from family. A society that highly values family and marriage and works out these values in practice reaps significant economic benefits. Foreigners are disconnected from the community of origin. Building and maintaining relationships with new community members is essential.

In response to biblical teaching, the development and operation of societal structures including government should consider their impact on the poor. Kingdoms infiltrated by the people of the Kingdom of Heaven can be shining examples reflecting God's heart for the powerless.

How does this all apply to governments in our contemporary context?

What is the role of government in relation to the poor? How could the influence of biblical principles work out in practice?

How can a government impact the poor for good? How can a government effectively mitigate the poverty resulting from sin?

The story of the sheep and goats in Matthew 25:31-46 makes it very clear that ultimately the nations will be judged by what they did with the poor, the sick and the socially disabled. Nations, not just individuals have a responsibility in this matter.

Some years ago, I attended a meeting called by the cooperative of organisations (both government and non-government) involved in social services in our city. The issue being discussed was the widening gap between the rich and the poor in our community. Four speakers addressed the meeting. The first speaker was a local school principal who described the need of struggling families in her school community. We all felt empathy with the solo-mother trying to feed and house her children. Then came the presentation of a social worker and tertiary teacher in social work. He spoke of the various other factors involved in the life of the poor in our community. In particular, he mentioned the common factor of 'social disconnectedness'. The last two people were actively involved in politics. The conservative politician, an economist, described the widening gap and the need to fix the increasing problem of the cost of housing. The fourth spoke about fixing the problem by increasing the redistribution of wealth through the state welfare system. Both of the latter speakers seemed to overlook addressing the cause and the nature of the problem which the first two speakers described.

Although governments cannot eliminate the problem, as

explained in a previous chapter, it behooves governments to do more than 'provide an ambulance at the bottom of the cliff'. Government policies and practices need to be more discerning, and address more than the symptoms of the problem.

In the light of the biblical identification of the poor to be widows, orphans and foreigners and the modern understanding of the role of social disconnectedness in poverty, it is clear that 'social poverty' must be considered when asking the question of what best can we do. The best welfare comes hand in hand with relationship building and relationship restoration. It includes relating to those who can mutually share love, wisdom and practical resources. It includes the most fundamental of relationships – with the One who is love and wisdom in person. A relationship with the Lord himself brings a deep understanding of identity, hope and destiny. Officers of an impersonal regulatory state struggle to build meaningful relationships with those whom they are helping. That is why the most effective channels of welfare are non-government agencies or private individuals and are often citizens of the kingdom of God. The church of Jesus Christ is the largest welfare NGO in the whole world. That is where you and I can step up to the plate.

Given that the core role of government is to affirm (encourage and enable) those who do good and punish (command and control) those who do wrong, governments can seek to find a way to:

- Affirm those who provide economic opportunity for the poor.

- Affirm families who remain positively connected and supportive of each other.
- Affirm families who ensure their children are educated to live economically and relationally fulfilling lives.
- Affirm those who care for and educate the poor.
- Punish those who exploit the vulnerable (e.g. abusive employers, money lenders, scammers etc).

These are just a few possible ways government can be involved.

When writing the first on this list, I am reminded of businessmen in Christian history who pioneered helping people get ahead in life. Examples include the Barclays, who established banks to enable people with an enterprise vision to get a start with seed finance, and the Cadbury family, who cared for their employees by providing rewarding working conditions and housing. There are modern examples of business entrepreneurs inspired by a 'social conscience'. A government can find ways to encourage and enable such enterprises.

Many governments in the free world have measures addressing these bullet points and more. It is an ongoing task to review and refine these measures to continue to achieve their intended goal.

State versus private welfare?

In the early twentieth century when governments began to develop the welfare state, some political leaders promoted it as putting Christianity into practice. Others resisted it, calling it practical socialism. Consequently, questions were asked. Is welfare the proper role of the state? Should the state's first priority be to affirm personal responsibility and work? Should the state find ways to affirm the family and the local community meeting the needs of the poor? The reality is these prior 'ports of call' are chronically falling short of the task, and so the state has become the necessary 'neighbour of last resort'. Sadly, the state can easily become 'the neighbour of first resort'. When this happens state welfare can become seen as an unconditional entitlement and can override personal, family and community responsibility.

A few years ago, a member of the New Zealand parliament revealed that when she was a beneficiary living in a state-provided house, she had her mother living with her. That was against the rules, and so her political opponents gave her a hard time. From my perspective it seems that she was doing the right thing, but the regulations were rewarding and so encouraging family disconnection! It is a challenge for a state to provide welfare while at the same time encourage personal responsibility and family connectedness. As it has been said many times, the art of politics is often some form of compromise! It will not achieve the ideal. It requires prayerful, creative lateral thinking!

Ultimately, governments, by working from the realm of the socio-political system, cannot completely fix the problem of poverty. While sin exists in humanity, this challenge will always be present. The best answer to poverty is the inside-out action of the Holy Spirit in our lives, the work of the King of the kingdom of heaven, restoring our relationship with Him, our family and community, and giving us the wisdom to use our resources effectively to enable flourishing of us all.

REFLECTIONS

Making Connection:

Read 2 Corinthians 5:16-21.

How are acts of welfare an essential part of the 'ministry of reconciliation'?

As one who has a degree of material wealth, how can you get socially connected to people who do not have wealth?

How can you learn from them and begin to share what you have (materially, educationally, experiential wisdom, and spiritually) with them?

How could a government help this sort of thing to happen more?

Serving in your specific vocation:

In what field of activity do you find yourself serving?

Do you know the gist of what the Bible says about it?

Do you need to learn more of what God's Word says about it?

Embark on a 'wisdom search' using the framework suggested in this chapter.

If you are a parent, ask yourself, what responsibility do I have to pass on this wisdom to my children?

Immigration:

In the light of the advice given in the law of Moses, the Torah, concerning the poor, widows and foreigners, the story of Ruth makes for a fascinating study of immigration policy. Read the book of Ruth.

Did Ruth choose to migrate with Naomi because she knew about the laws regarding people in her position imbedded into the Israelite culture?

Does her choice to make Israel her people-group and the LORD her God signal the most successful way to migrate to a more successful and hospitable country?

Does this story stir you as a believer to consider how you could serve immigrants?

13

WHAT IS IT ABOUT CIVIL GOVERNMENT THAT MATTERS?

Often when people in the free world think about civil government, they think that it's democracy that matters. For them the bottom-line question is: "Is it democratic?"

Is it 'democracy' that matters? If democracy matters, what is it about democracy that matters?

In answering these questions, this chapter pulls together ideas from previous chapters and presents a summary of some of the main ideas in this book, and suggests what we should do in response to it.

Ideologically driven?

Much of the political life in the 20th century and since, has been characterised by assumed values and trends such as:

- the continued belief in the nation state,
- the value of economic growth and production,
- the rapid advance in technology, along with

- the progressive rejection of the moral values derived from the Judeo-Christian ethic and meta-narrative, and
- the increase in the power of the state through rules and regulations.

What undergirds such assumptions and trends?

These days we often hear politicians criticising their opponents with the accusation that their policies and practices are ideologically driven. I am still waiting for a repost like this:

"Yes, in this matter we are ideologically driven, and confidently so! The idea and the values behind this policy are..."

All political action is driven by an ideology. Some are aware of the ideology underpinning their policies and practice. Some are not, being unaware that they have assumed certain ideas and values. C.S. Lewis is often quoted, although it is not certain that he said it in these exact words, "The most dangerous ideas in a society are not the ones being argued, but the ones being assumed." Being unaware of the ideology that shapes their thinking is very precarious, particularly when in a position of influence or power. They are not in control of the direction their decisions are taking them. They can finish up being driven by the ideas that are prevalent or are being pushed upon contemporary society and thus doing the will of whoever has the loudest voice shouting in their ear!

I have heard some, including politicians, say they are evidential, rather than religiously or philosophically based. They claim to believe only what research reveals to be true. That stance is a philosophical or ideological position, based on the belief that scientific research is the only source of knowledge or truth. It is called scientism or empiricism. Unfortunately for empiricists, scientific research will never answer some basic questions of human life. It cannot tell us what is right or wrong, or what is the ultimate purpose or meaning of life. These shape the very foundations of governmental decision-making.

Some politicians say they are not following any philosophical, religious or political ideology. They say they seek to find out and apply what works. Such people are called pragmatists. This begs the question, "When they say it works, it works to do what? What are the criteria to determine what works? What is the purpose that defines what they want to achieve?" That purpose, that goal is derived from a value, and that value comes from a 'worldview' which consciously or unconsciously shapes their decision-making. Pragmatism is a dangerous ideology. It idolises the 'means' while overlooking the end to which it is leading. We all need to be alert to the trap of only concerning ourselves with 'the how' and neglecting to reflect on 'the why'.

This book has attempted to describe the aspects of a worldview or ideology that have come from the Bible and which are applicable to civil government. In short, this is: that belief in a Sovereign Creator and Sustainer of the universe who has spoken through prophets and the person and work of Jesus Christ leads to a set of values that have enabled the rise and continuance of the civilisation we commonly call the free world.

Social cohesion

Sometimes we hear politicians appealing to common sense. This is attractive to people who have an instinctive sense of what is sensible. However, this fails to appreciate that one's sense of what is reasonable can be different from that of one's neighbours. Our 'common sense' is not necessarily common when there is a divergent sense of what is of value and what is right and wrong.

People involved in government often say that social cohesion is our greatest asset. This raises the question: We need to ask what is the foundation of social cohesion? Social cohesion depends upon the people sharing common values. Without a common acceptance of values, and the discipline of much of the population to live by them, this system of freedom we have come to call 'democracy' is in jeopardy.

Social synergy functions on a commitment to shared values which are held despite our differences. Shared values come from a common story in which to live. This metanarrative or worldview must be cogent and believable, and it must be livable; that is, applicable to all of life. Sometimes this is referred to as 'social capital'. If these values are abandoned, the socio-political structures that depend on them are in peril.

A society is like a piece of fabric. In the Western world, the articulation of the common values holding the social fabric together has been done by the church. The people of the kingdom of God have been like agents of the 'Master Weaver'. Attending to the breaches in the social fabric, civil government has taken the role of the 'darners', doing temporary repairs to the social order.

The politics of the West has seen 'left' and 'right' wing parties. Often one 'wing' has prioritised economic freedom and the other prioritised social equity. When there has existed a common commitment to a higher authority or set of values, there has been a degree of respect for each other. The system, with its swings left and right, has worked reasonably smoothly. But when that common sense of accountability and shared values is absent, there has been a greater degree of polarisation and mutual disrespect, and anger is expressed when there is a change of government. The system has shown signs of faltering.

In 1948, Jaques Ellul wrote:

> In order for people to understand each other they need a minimum of shared ideas, biases, and values, which are usually held unconsciously ... [When something else destroys this common fund] ... Other biases are probably created, other shared ideas, but they have other characteristics. Instead of being the deepest and most authentic expression of a particular civilisation, they now are the myths and artificial ideas created by propaganda. (Ellul, 2016, p.75)

Seventy plus years later we observe how this has played out. We observe an increasing occurrence of disrespect, family breakdown, violent crime, poverty, addiction, sexual abuse, and political polarisation. These threaten the cohesion of our civilisation. This trend has not resulted solely from government policy and practice – it has continued regardless of the particular government of the time. Rather, it is the result of a progressive rejection of the beliefs and values stemming from the Judeo-Christian worldview. One generation turns away from the Christian faith, the source of the values they are deeply committed to. The next generation adopts a different set of values. Christianity is relegated to historical myth, and instead a disparate range of values is promoted. We find ourselves in the context of a new enlightenment or social awareness. This is sometimes called by its critics as 'wokeness'. It involves the pursuit of values that are often antagonistic to God's values, and that lead to decline of the social fabric rather than flourishing.

> Where there is no revelation (or vision),
> people cast off restraint. (Proverbs 29:18)

A notable consequence of this is that there are political parties, on both 'the left' and 'the right', that have lost sight of the Judeo-Christian worldview in the context of which they were founded. They have lost their way, with policies that are not rooted in their foundational values. People are reticent to vote for a leadership that lacks a clear vision and commitment to principles and action that will enable the common good. These parties desperately need to revisit their original vision. In the light of these principles and values, they should re-evaluate and if necessary remake, their current policies and practices.

Righteous self-governance

The biblical narrative relates God's pleasure or displeasure with governors, kings or governments. God's approval is not dependent on the political structure – the degree of structural 'democracy', but rather on the degree of integrity – how faithful the government is to God-given values and to acting to fulfil the purpose of the common good of the people. Lack of this integrity is called corruption. Sadly, we see corruption rife in the governments of many nations around the world. This is the greatest impediment of stable government and of social justice.

As noted in this book, a key to social justice and good government is the righteousness or self-governance of the citizens and their leaders. Without a significant degree of self-governance, a society needs (and sometime seeks) a strong man or authoritarian government to rule 'with a rod of iron', along with all the lack of freedom and injustices that can come with that. The best-fit government, in terms of the degree of social control needed, is largely determined by the degree of virtue and wisdom (self-governance) of the people.

In times of crisis such as war, a nation needs authoritative, decisive leadership. Meanwhile, in the regular times, God gives a nation a government which best fits their virtue and wisdom as this diagram attempts to express graphically:

Degree of government control

absolute authoritarian ⟵――――――――――⟶ small human government

foolish and sinful   wise and virtuous

Degree of righteousness of the people

It appears that God gives an undisciplined people an authoritative government to keep them in order. The freedoms that come with smaller government and the accompanying prosperity are dependent on the degree of self-governance of the people. A nation with people who have little commitment to the principles and values that come from the Bible cannot sustain a form of government which affords a greater degree of freedom. The second president of America (one of the framers of the constitution), John Adams, is widely quoted saying:

> We have no government in power capable of contending with human passions unbridled by morality and religion... Our constitution was made only for a moral and religious people. It is wholly inadequate to the government of any other. (From: 'letters to the officers of the first brigade of the third division of the militia of Massachusetts', October 1798)

This was the prevailing belief of the people who established America. Freedom is dependent on the righteousness of Christ.

The keys to self-governance are:

Virtue: The will and resolution to do what is good, for the benefit of others. This is a spiritual and moral matter, a matter of motivation.

> offer your bodies [whole beings] as a living sacrifice, holy and pleasing to God... (Romans 12:1)

This is putting God as Lord of life, individually and corporately. This is being determined to wholeheartedly do whatever God says is good. This is a matter of our 'heart' commitment to God.

Wisdom: Knowing what is good and how to do it. This is an educational matter, a matter of the mind.

> Do not be conformed to the pattern of this world but be transformed by the renewing of your mind. Then you will be able to test and approve what God's will is. (Romans 12:2)

An understanding of what is good and what is evil comes from God's revelation, not from a self-determined idea of right and wrong. Remember, "The fear of the LORD is the beginning of wisdom" (Psalms 111:10, Proverbs 1:7, Proverbs 9:10). This is a matter of the mind – the 'head' following the heart commitment.

Service: Humbly putting into practice what God has called us to do. This is a practical matter, a matter of action.

> Each of you should use whatever gift you have received to serve others, as faithful stewards of God's grace in its various forms. (See 1 Peter 4:10, and Romans 12:3ff)

This is a matter of our 'hands' – our heart attitude made visible by our action.

What we seek are principles of the kingdom of heaven implanted within individuals and worked out into all of life – the inside-out work of the Holy Spirit. Let us aspire to righteousness!

> Blessed are those who hunger and thirst for righteousness for they shall be filled. (Matthew 5:6)

Seek to rightly relate to God as king, and He will fill you with His ideas. Seek to do what is right, and you will be filled with confidence to do it. Seek to rightly deal with people justly and you will be filled with the gratitude of others.

So, what is it about democracy that matters?

Hence we come to the question at the heart of this book: What is it about civil government that matters most? It is not necessarily the political structure that matters most. It is not whether it is a republic or a constitutional monarchy. It is not the degree of representation of the various groups in society. It is not the electoral system used. It is not whether private capitalism or state capitalism is promoted.

What really matters is:

- A common commitment to the values that respect everyone as made in the image of God, and to the ideology or worldview from which these values come.
- Heeding what God says is good and evil.
- The self-discipline of the people to do what is right.
- The integrity of the leadership to consistently do what is right for the common good.
- The influence of people who have a restored relationship with God and so are committed to self-giving love.
- Serving God by serving others.
- The kingdom of God worked out in the lives of the citizens.

In short, it is righteousness!

Yes, it is righteousness that exalts a nation (Proverbs 14:34). Its effect in a nation is far-reaching.

For example, when righteousness has sway in the lives of people, work is a means of serving others to the glory of God. Private enterprise becomes a means of providing quality goods and services, fulfilling work for employees. Work gives people the capacity to do things to benefit others. When righteousness is lived out, more families hold together and there is less need for the charity of others. When righteousness is pervasive, less government expenditure is needed to punish or restrict those who do wrong and more can be directed toward rewarding those who do right.

On the other hand, unrighteousness incurs oppression and conflict. With less righteousness, society needs more controls. A 'free' society moves toward collapse. With more righteousness, society moves toward a greater flourishing of all – the common good, the 'shalom' of the people.

How do we start to do the part that we specifically can play?

In the light of the above, what should we do? To answer this question, Psalm 32 is worth reading. It gives apt advice.

The first step toward righteousness is to recognise our own unrighteousness and repent, turn away from our shortcomings and put our faith in Christ who imputes us with His righteousness. Once we make Him our leader, our king, we can say with the Psalmist, "He leads me in the paths of righteousness" (Psalm 23:3). We are then able to outwork our salvation (our wholeness) in our relationships with others in the public sphere.

Next, pray for all people and in particular governments, who can enable environments where people are free to speak the truth of the kingdom of heaven and thus people can respond and be set free to do good and live flourishing lives.

I urge, then, first of all, that petitions, prayers, intercession and thanksgiving be made for all people – for kings and all those in authority, that we may live peaceful and quiet lives in all godliness and holiness. This is good, and pleases God our Saviour, who wants all people to be saved and to come to a knowledge of the truth. (1 Timothy 2:1-4)

This is the kingdom of heaven at work. As we pray we listen, and the LORD can guide us as to what to specifically do.

The LORD seeks to build His kingdom through us. Each do their part in responding to His calling, working for the kingdom of heaven, shaping in some way the lives of others. We will not see how it all fits together until, at the resurrection and the restoration of all things, His kingdom will be revealed – brought into fruition for all to see. Meanwhile, we are called to be 'salt' in our community and nation, preserving the very fabric of our world by our self-sacrificing love.

Each citizen of the kingdom of heaven has a part to play! The work of the kingdom is done by the meek, the merciful, the pure in heart, the persecuted, outworking the grace of God to others. God's sovereignty with our cooperation will bring about the kingdom of God.

What is your particular part in building for the kingdom?
The calling of God is not just our paid or voluntary 'work'. It is for all of our life. It is an integral part of our identity, rooted in our relationship with God. It includes our regular 'employment', and other things you do for the benefit of others. This may be as part of the work initiated by your local church or it may be something you do with the support of fellow believers.

We all are gifted differently by the Holy Spirit to contribute our unique part in the work for His kingdom.

To each one the observable outworking of the Spirit is given for the common good. (See 1 Corinthians 12:7)

Here are some possibilities. We may be involved in several or many of these:

- Express gratitude to a neighbour for something they do or have done.
- Tell the story of Christ to others so they can respond and begin their journey of relationship with God.
- Introduce people to Jesus who imputes righteousness to those who believe in Him.
- Inspire and train your children to love God in all that they do in their lives.
- Communicate the glory of God with works of art, music or literature.
- Care for an old or dying person as a nurse or visitor to hospital.
- Mentor a foreign student with practical help. Our action may lead them to ask why we do it. We can tell them the story of Jesus.
- Assist in the distribution of food and clothing to those in need.
- In a time of community crisis, volunteer or mobilise a team of volunteers to meet the needs of people.
- Support refugees and guide them in the practical

things they need to know and do to live in your country, and introduce them to the beliefs and values that have made this nation so attractive. Tell stories that show how God has been at work.
- Create or provide quality goods to enhance the lives of others.
- Provide fulfilling employment for people in your community.
- Provide an essential service for the homeless or disabled.
- Teach your children, students and others in your life the Word of God and how to respond, to live it out every day.
- Use your online presence (e.g. on social media) to communicate the gospel and how the biblical story stacks up logically and experientially. (Make sure you keep it positive. Don't use it to be reactionary or judgmental.)
- Invest in a project to develop housing for Christian workers, refugees, and others in need of accommodation.
- Design inspiring and useful architecture that contributes to the wellbeing of the community who will use it.
- Individually, and as a church, encourage and inspire others to make a difference in the community to the glory of God.
- Set an example by being involved in voluntary public service.

- Help disabled people in practical ways such as transport and household chores.
- Relate to community leaders and politicians and encourage them in their work.
- Be involved in local government or political action guided by principles described in this book.
- Work in the public service, doing it unto God and not just the government.
- Build quality housing for people to live in as a service to the glory of God.
- Serve your family and neighbours in practical work to the glory of God.

In all of these and more, as you are led by the Spirit, you are contributing to the outworking of the kingdom of God, taking dominion in His kingdom as we were originally commissioned to do.

> Whatever you do, work at it with all your heart, as working for the Lord, not for human masters. (Colossians 3:23)

Working together, we will make an eternal difference, in this life and the life to come.

> Seek first His kingdom and His righteousness, and all these things [the resources for human flourishing] will be given to you as well. (Matthew 6:33)

In practice, in word and deed, let us live as citizens of the kingdom of God, contributing to the righteousness that will make our nation great for the glory of God.

REFLECTIONS

Cultural Christianity/righteousness:

Clearly, Christianity can have a profound positive effect on the culture of a nation.

Why is this not a good reason to adopt Christianity?

How does choosing Christianity for utilitarian purposes such as this miss the whole point of the Christian faith?

Making a nation more 'Christian':

> Papua New Guinea is officially a Christian country. The preamble to its constitution has been amended to "acknowledge and declare God, the Father; Jesus Christ, the Son; and Holy Spirit, as our Creator and Sustainer of the entire universe and the source of our powers and authorities, delegated to the people and all persons within the geographical jurisdiction of Papua New Guinea." Prime Minister James Marape, a Seventh-day Adventist, said Christianity is an essential anchor for the country's national identity. Some Christian lead-

ers there have expressed hope that the change will help bring national harmony and advance efforts to end violence and corruption. Others, such as Catholic bishop Giorgio Licini, warn it will likely lead to disillusionment. The constitutional change has not altered guarantees of religious freedom. (*Christianity Today*, September/October 2025)

What *can* be done to increase the wisdom and virtue of a nation?

Outworked Christianity/righteousness:

Consider your part in outworking the kingdom of heaven in the context of the community, city and nation in which you are located. Individually, or in a small group, clarify what God would have you do in this context. Walk through the steps below together. In the light of what Christ has achieved for you, prayerfully examine your strategy in fulfilling God's calling for you. Listen to the Holy Spirit as you pray.

Step 1: Read Romans 12:1 and the section under the heading Virtue in this chapter. Recommit to do what God has called you to do.

Step 2: Read Romans 12:2 and the section under the heading Wisdom in this chapter. Ask God to give you the wisdom to know and do what is His will, what is right in your current family, work, church and community context.

Step 3: Read Romans 12:3-8 and the section under the heading Service in this chapter. With confident humility, examine what your God-given abilities and motivations are. How can these be used to serve in the various contexts of your life?

Now, in the spirit of the rest of Romans 12, with humble confidence, encouraging one another: *do it!*

GROUP DISCUSSION STARTER GUIDE

The following is a list of many statements related to ideas addressed in this book. They are a mixture of statements which are blatantly right, blatantly wrong or are subject to dispute. They are designed to provoke discussion and raise questions which may be answered (or not) by the reading of this book. They can evoke a range of reactions in a group, and so can test the grace of the members of a discussion group. I suggest, if you are a discussion leader, choose a small selection (not all of them!) and, relating to each statement, ask such questions as:

How does this statement line up with biblical principles?

How should I reflect on and change my way of thinking and acting in the light of the biblical truth?

How should I deal with my reaction to people who think differently to me on this matter?

How should I relate to the Lord about this matter?

What action to promote the kingdom of heaven is God prompting me to do?

Discussion starter statements related to the topic of this book:

1. When there is a problem in society, the government should fix it.

2. Making the incomes of its citizens as equal as possible should be one of the top priorities of any legitimate government.

3. The purpose of the legal system is to eliminate offence in society by rehabilitating offenders.

4. God puts in place only governments which follow His principles.

5. Under some circumstances, Christians are called to disobey the laws of the government.

6. When you study the Bible as a whole, it becomes clear that God is very supportive of an economic system that is based on private property, the work ethic, and personal responsibility.

7. Making as much money as you can is more important than whether you have a good reputation.

8. The bottom-line purpose of any business is to make a profit, especially for the shareholders.

9. Internet providers should censor hate speech.

10. The best tax system would be one based on a flat tax system where everyone pays the same percentage of their income in taxes.

11. The Bible states that money is the root of all evil.

12. It is the responsibility of the government to create wealth.

13. Physically and mentally healthy adults who do not work should not be protected from suffering the consequences of their actions.

14. Science, history, literature and educational skills and facts can be taught without a religious or philosophical foundation.

15. Our moral decisions should be based only on reliable research.

16. The government should require that only a licensed teacher be permitted to teach or instruct a child in an educational setting.

17. Values clarification courses or situational ethics should be taught to students in our educational system.

18. The government should require students to pass a prescribed national test before graduating from high school.

19. The government should pass legislation allowing doctors and family members to decide when a loved one should be able to choose how they die based on the individual's quality of life.

20. Since it is her body, a woman should be free to end her pregnancy with an abortion.

22. Since God is not the author of law, the author of law must be man. In other words, the law is the law simply because the highest human authority, which is the state, has said it is law and is able to back it up by force.

23. The separation of church and state must be enforced, prohibiting the acknowledgment of God in the public schools, governmental buildings, meetings and property.

24. Our judicial system should allow judges, through their decisions and rulings, to guide and shape the foundational basis of law.

25. Originally, the Ten Commandments provided the basis for our legal and political system, creating justice and peace.

26. You can't legislate morality. Legislating morality is a violation of the separation of church and state.

27. If there is to be moral and legal order, there must be absolutes.

28. The government should fund school-based health clinics which would include safe-sex counselling.

29. Every person who has ever lived on earth, except Adam and Eve and Jesus Christ, was born with a propensity to grievously sin.

30. Salvation is a gift from God that cannot be earned or achieved by good legislation.

31. Both Secular Humanism and Marxism are religious worldviews.

32. The Bible is God's revealed Word and should be the basis of our worldview and legal system.

33. Believers should not only base their philosophy in Christ, but they should know how to respond to the critics and sceptics of Christianity with the reasoning and basis of our biblical worldview.

34. A Christian can develop a biblical worldview for every major area of life by studying the Bible from beginning to end in context.

35. There is a Bible verse that states that God helps those who help themselves.

36. It is the government's responsibility to define what marriage is.

37. Ultimately, every individual will bow their knee and confess with their mouth that Jesus Christ is Lord.

38. One of the Ten Commandments is You shalt not kill. Thus, it stands to reason that God is opposed to war and nations going to war.

39. Marriage is not legitimate without a state-issued certificate.

40. Family, church and state are institutions ordained by God.

41. If the research and theory of a group of scientists contradicts the Word of God, the error is with the scientists, not the Bible.

42. Truth is discovered by man, not created by man.

43. One of the greatest virtues one can possess is the virtue of tolerance, namely, we accept everyone's lifestyles as equal.

44. The Bible says, judge not lest you be judged, which means we are not to judge the choices or behaviour of a person as right or wrong. We all make mistakes, and thus we should

not judge someone's actions or behaviour according to any particular standard.

45. Biblically minded Christians should look at the issues of the world as falling into one of two categories, the secular and the sacred.

46. If it 'works' for you, then it must be true.

47. Pastors and Christians who speak out publicly against homosexuality should be prosecuted for hate speech and a hate crime.

48. Popular music is demonic.

49. Music is a way to invoke the blessing of God.

50. The biblical purpose for wealth is to provide for one's family, proclaim the Gospel, be a blessing to others, test one's stewardship and one's loyalty to God.

51. Immigration should be limited to those who choose to do what Ruth in the Bible did – commit to the worldview and the values of the country.

52. Christians should set aside their beliefs when they play sport.

53. A God given responsibility of government is to protect the righteous and punish the wicked.

54. People with genetic diseases should be sterilised.

55. Your worldview is the foundation of your values and your values are the foundation of your actions.

56. Doing God's will day by day is more important than whether we live or die.

57. The Bible is a consistent revelation from beginning to end. It is a reflection of God's character and nature.

APPENDIX

The New Zealand National Anthem

E Ihowā Atua
O ngā iwi mātou rā
Āta whakarangona
Me aroha noa.
Kia hua ko te pai
Kia tau tō atawhai
Manaakitia mai
Aotearoa.

God of Nations at Thy feet
In the bonds of love we meet
Hear our voices, we entreat
God defend our free land.
Guard Pacific's triple star
From the shafts of strife and war
Make her praises heard afar
God defend New Zealand.

Men of every creed and race
Gather here before Thy face

Asking Thee to bless this place
God defend our free land.
From dissension, envy, hate
And corruption guard our state
Make our country good and great
God defend New Zealand.

Peace, not war, shall be our boast
But, should foes assail our coast
Make us then a mighty host
God defend our free land.
Lord of battles in Thy might
Put our enemies to flight
Let our cause be just and right
God defend New Zealand.

Let our love for Thee increase
May Thy blessings never cease
Give us plenty, give us peace
God defend our free land.
From dishonour and from shame
Guard our country's spotless name
Crown her with immortal fame
God defend New Zealand.

May our mountains ever be
Freedom's ramparts on the sea
Make us faithful unto Thee
God defend our free land.
Guide her in the nations' van

Preaching love and truth to man
Working out Thy glorious plan
God defend New Zealand.

FOR FURTHER READING

As said in the preface, this book is not intended to be a comprehensive analysis of either what the Bible says on this topic, how it has worked out in history, or its application to the public life of the Christian. Rather, it is a brief and simple introduction to the topic, in the hope that it will provoke both further investigation and a renewed pursuit of making a difference for the kingdom of God. With that in mind, here is an introductory list of some of the books on this topic that I have found informative and inspirational. They are in order of publication date.

Books that focus on biblical foundations

Ellul, J. (1970). *The Meaning of the City*, Eerdmans Publishing.

Schaeffer, F.A. (1983). *How Should We Then Live? The rise and decline of western thought and culture*. Crossway Books.

Bickel, B., & Jantz, S. (2003). *Why Jesus Matters*. Barbour Publishing.

McIlroy, D. (2004). *A Biblical View of Law and Justice.* Paternoster Press.

Mangalwadi, V. (2011). *The Book that Made Your World: How the Bible created the soul of western civilization.* Thomas Nelson Inc.

Holland, T. (2019). *Dominion: How the Christian Revolution Remade the World.* Basic Books.

Ellul, J. (2016). *Presence in the Modern World: A new translation by Lisa Richmond.* Cascade Books. This book was originally written (in French) in 1948, and first translated into English as *The Presence of the Kingdom* in 1967.

Wright, T. (2016). *God in Public: How the Bible speaks truth to power today.* The Society for Promoting Christian Knowledge.

Books that focus more on practical application

Monsma, S.V. (with Larry Baldock) (1984). *Pursuing Justice in a Sinful World: Revised New Zealand edition.* Eerdmans Publishing.

Volf, M. (2011). *A Public Faith.* Brazos Press.

Ashford, B. (2015). *Every Square Inch: An introduction to cultural engagement for Christians.* Lexham Press.

Volf, M. & McAnnally-Linz, R. (2016) *Public Faith in Action: How to engage with commitment, conviction, and courage.* Brazos Press.

Wright, N.T., & Bird, M.F. (2024). *Jesus and the Powers.* The Society for Promoting Christian Knowledge.

Video series about how the message of Jesus Christ has changed the world

Faase K. *Jesus the Game Changer.* Olive Tree Media Limited, Australia. Season 1 is a ten-part documentary series on how the life and teaching of Jesus changed the world and why it matters. It comes with a discussion guide, so that it can be used in settings such as churches, small groups and schools.

Organisations producing media promoting the intelligent engagement of Christianity in contemporary culture and the public square

Thinking Matters New Zealand is a service encouraging Christians to explore what they believe and why they believe it so they can engage culture and present the Christian faith with gentleness and respect. thinkingmatters.org.nz

The Centre for Public Christianity (CPX), a media organisation based in Australia, offers a Christian perspective on contemporary life and culture. publicchristianity.org

The Venn Foundation, an educational institution that helps people embrace the riches of Scripture and the Christian tradition for the good of their homes, workplaces, universities, churches, and communities. venn.org.nz

ALSO BY JOHN NORSWORTHY

Norsworthy, J. (2009). *Why Culture Matters: A biblical Christian approach to things cultural.* ConsultEd Publishing.

Norsworthy, J. (2014). *Educating Our Children Faithfully: The story of the New Zealand Christian school movement, 1964-2014.* New Zealand Association for Christian Schools.

Norsworthy, J. (2018). *Why Science Matters: What does the Bible say about things scientific?* ConsultEd Publishing.

Norsworthy, J. (2021). *Why Humility Matters: The radical idea of the practice of humility.* ConsultEd Publishing.

www.ingramcontent.com/pod-product-compliance
Lightning Source LLC
Chambersburg PA
CBHW071957290426
44109CB00018B/2055